## Praise for *Divine Laughter*

"Karl and Rolf Jacobson have performed a miracle by creating a book about humor, the Bible, and preaching that is genuinely witty and at the same time profound. Almost every page of this book evokes rich laughter, but as is the case with the best humor, the laughter erupts from a sudden shift in perspective and with the gift of surprising insight. The Jacobson brothers understand the gospel itself as the promise that God's grace will get the last laugh, and therefore, they guide us toward preaching that is more humble, more humane, and more joyful."

—**Thomas G. Long**, Bandy Professor Emeritus of Preaching, Candler School of Theology

"They say one should never, ever attempt to analyze humor. I would amend that to say, never attempt it *unless you have God on your side*. Pastors Karl and Rolf Jacobson examine God's word and discover that there is much joy and, yes, humor there. A fun, serious, and seriously fun book!"

—**Bridget Jones and Mike Nelson**, Rifftrax.com / Mystery Science Theater 3000

"Perhaps we are so solemn in church because we suspect there is so little at stake that we must dignify with soberness and somberness. The brothers Jacobson know better. They know that there is so much at stake—so outrageous and so risky for God and for the world—that we need both the relief and the side-angle of humor. They bring to their work a deep reading of Scripture, deep rootage in the tradition, and a deep love for the church. It does not matter if the name of the 'older brother' was Karl or Rolf. Both are invited to the party of hilarious fun. You will not want to miss it either!"

—**Walter Brueggemann**, Columbia Theological Seminary

"I've long suspected that heresy in the pulpit is a far less worrisome problem than dullness. *Divine Laughter* equips us to offer sermons that are both interesting and invigorating by developing a biblical understanding of the power of humor to invite us to laugh at our ourselves, to be surprised and delighted by the joy of the gospel, and to call into question a cultural reality that falls far short of the abundant life God offers. This book is *not* about telling jokes, but rather rediscovering the courageous and life-giving power of humor that is rooted in the ultimate joke God plays on death and the devil in the resurrection of Christ. Buy it, read it, laugh with (and even at!) its authors, and be renewed and encouraged in your calling."

—**David J. Lose**, senior pastor, Mount Olivet Lutheran Church, and author of *Preaching at the Crossroads*

# DIVINE LAUGHTER

# DIVINE LAUGHTER

*Preaching and the Serious Business of Humor*

KARL N. JACOBSON AND

ROLF A. JACOBSON

*Foreword by Will Willimon*

Fortress Press
Minneapolis

DIVINE LAUGHTER
Preaching and the Serious Business of Humor



Cover design: Emily Harris Designs / Kristin Miller

Print ISBN: 978-1-5064-6867-9
eBook ISBN: 978-1-5064-6868-6

For the Boys of Sommer Ro:

Darrell, David, Hans, Mark, Mike, and Tim

# CONTENTS

# FOREWORD

Hear the one about the two Lutheran pastor/scholars who wandered into the Bible and found mirth, sarcasm, jokes and jibes, puns, and fun where the rest of us thought there was only insufferable, stolid prudishness?

If all Old Testament scholars were as fun as the Jacobson boys, I'd have taken more Old Testament courses in seminary, and we'd all be reading and proclaiming the Bible more faithfully.

Egged on by the brothers Jacobson, I'll at last admit it: for years I've slipped into comedy clubs incognito. Watching a comic stand and deliver, forming strangers into a community with nothing but words, using biting social commentary and critique and having people laugh as they pay good money for it rather than storm out in rage because of it. Now that's a preacher's dream.

"What line of work are you in, Bud, and what brings you to Chicago?" asked the perfect stranger seated next to me, the big guy who was laughing so hard that tears were rolling down his pink cheeks, his arm around me, even though before the comic's routine we couldn't make eye contact.

"Me? Er, uh, Art Vandelay. I'm in export/import," I lied with a grin.

To the young comic who was busy making strangers into family, I whispered, *Teach me how to do what you're doing*. Not in a comedy club in Chicago but in a pulpit in Durham.

As someone who weekly works in words, not from a stage in a comedy club in Chicago, but in drab Durham from a pulpit, attempting to move people from where they are to where God wants them to be, to get them to take a sober look at themselves from a comedic point of view, like the prophets (major and minor) assaulting the received world with nothing but words, I've always felt comradery with stand-up comics, though I doubt Jerry Seinfeld thinks the same about me.

So along come Karl and Rolf Jacobson marveling at the fun side of Scripture. Sure, I knew that Jonah was a good joke, but Job? Who has ever cracked a smile while reading the Psalms? The Jacobsons, that's who. Even Jesus loved to tell a good joke to us, otherwise known as a parable. And you thought that Amos's only stab at humor was his fat "cows of Bashan" (Amos 4:1).

Without even once committing what I consider to be the unforgiveable sin (namely, dullness), these guys show that only humor can handle the serious truth of the topsy-turvy gospel. Jokes trade in surprise, delight, and love to humble, to make humane. The Jacobsons demonstrate that there's no way to talk about the reckless salvation in Jesus Christ without sometimes having to smile, without the holy humbling that comes when we realize that the joke is on us. The God whom we gave ample cause to weep, otherwise known as Jesus Christ, instead smiles.

Hear the one about the God who got mixed up with frail, fickle, flawed humanity and paid dearly for it, the baby born into the world he created, the omnipotent one who allowed himself to be pushed out of his creation on a cross, and who retaliated by returning to and forgiving his murderers? The punch line none of us stuffed shirts expected, otherwise known as resurrection. It's enough to make you laugh.

"You guys will be the death of me," he said to his knuckleheaded disciples. With a grin? Let's hope so.

A warning to those of you who are preachers: hang out with the Jacobson boys and you may wind up in trouble. I've never had difficulty with a congregation for being too serious in a sermon. Humor—particularly when ventured among the dour, oh-so-serious-to-the-point-of-deadly faithful—can be at our expense. Though Easter was the great joke that God played on the Devil, we are prone to take ourselves and our good works too seriously. (Not a bad definition of sin.)

Another thing: preacher, never tell a joke in a sermon, never mock the proud and powerful or stoop to the use of sarcasm, ridicule, or satire—unless God does.

Thanks, Jacobsons, we needed this.

*Will Willimon*

# INTRODUCTION

You might expect us to start with a joke. It's a book about humor (yes, *and* preaching) after all.[1] But before we get to the punch line, we want to start with something actually devoid of humor—something sad, tragic even.

When it comes to reading the Bible—and then talking with someone about it, preaching on it, and so on—have you ever felt like you're not on the same page? Or, worse yet, that you're on the same page, but it feels like you're reading a totally different book?

We have.

When people only read certain parts of the Old Testament and then say that the God of the Old Testament is not the same as the God of the New Testament . . .

Or when some earnest believer tries to read the stories of Jonah or of Shadrach, Meshach, and Abednego, or one of Jesus's parables in exactly the same way (read: *literally*) as they would the Ten Commandments or the Sermon on the Mount . . .

Or when we are told that there is no humor in the Bible, because it is about such serious stuff.

Humor and the stuff of faith come together far more frequently than we might think, and in far stranger places than we might dream of in our humorless philosophies or humorless faiths.

Religion, religious people, religious practices, and yes, even religious texts—Scripture, the Bible—both contain humor and can benefit from humor-filled engagement.

The Bible itself tells us that preaching and the Bible ought to bring humor, joy, and laughter to life. Check out how the book of Nehemiah talks about Scripture, interpretation, and preaching:

> So they read from the book, from the law of God, with interpretation. They gave the sense so that the people understood the reading.
>
> And Nehemiah, who was the governor, and Ezra the priest and scribe, and the Levites who taught the people said to them all, "This day is holy to the Lord your God; do not mourn or weep." For all of the people wept when they heard the words of the law. He said to them, "Go your way, eat the fat and drink wine and send portions of each to those for whom nothing is prepared, for this day is holy to our Lord; do not be grieved, for the joy of the Lord is your strength." So the Levites stilled all the people, saying, "Be quiet, for this day is holy; do not be grieved." And all the people went on their way to eat and drink and to share portions and did so with great mirth because they had understood the words that were taught to them. (8:8–12; our translation)

"With great mirth" instead of mourning or weeping or grieving! (Despite those grim Levites wanting them to be quiet about it.) Hearing the law, and understanding it, they were inclined to be filled with grief and sorrow but were surprised by mirth—joy-filled laughter at the goodness and mercy of their God.

It's like Martin Luther said: "When we should cry because of our sin, we laugh."[2] Now there is a description of a truthful and joyful life of faith made possible through the good humor of Christ Jesus!

The Bible is frequently funny, and we should let it be what it is. The content of the book out of which our proclamation arises needs our attention, and taking seriously [*sic*] the points at which the Bible is funny is important. This is true both in terms of how the Bible can create meaning for us and in terms of how we who read and preach the Bible can then preach it more fully.

What follows in this book is a serious [*double sic*] look at humor and laughter in the Bible. We will explore the theological implications of what it means if we think of God, Jesus, and even the Holy Spirit as filled with laughter. You are invited to wonder at and chuckle your way through examples of God's laughter in the Bible, thinking about what that means for God's people, for the life of faith, and for preaching to God's people.

As we will see, there is a serious [*triple sic*] variety of kinds of laughter in the Bible: laughter of surprise, joy, simple pleasure, derision and ridicule, and more. We explore, with no small measure of good humor of our own, these different kinds of laughter and the different laughers who laugh them.

There is even laughter and humor among the most seriously serious [*now that's just sick*] of biblical writers and speakers—the prophets. It may surprise us, but prophetic discourse employs a wide range of humorous techniques: sarcasm, parody, irony, satire, scorn. Specific prophetic oracles and sayings cannot be properly understood without taking this tone or style of delivery into consideration. If we fail to recognize humor at work in certain passages from the prophets, our reading of them will be profit-less (sorry, not sorry for that there).

This, then, is our invitation to you, dear preacher, as you think about your calling to proclaim God's word: do so with an eye to humor, an ear, heart, and mind attuned to sacred silliness, and a mouth filled with biblical laughter. As the great hymn paraphrase of Psalm 100 has it,

> All people that on earth do dwell,
> sing to the Lord with cheerful voice:
> *him serve with mirth*, his praise forth tell,
> come ye before him and rejoice. (Ps 100:1–2)

* * *

Projects such as this book don't fall out of the sky or tumble off the keyboard. They don't so much take work as take time. They take a lot of time in conversation with each other, with friends, and with colleagues. For better or worse, both of us tend to cope with life's absurdities and joys through laughter and humor. We think laughter and humor work better than anger. Thanks to all who have laughed with us over the years, especially our wives Amy and Angela and our children Thursday, Sam, Lucy, Nora, Claire, Ingrid, and Gunnar. This project began as a workshop that Karl gave a number of years ago at Luther Seminary's Celebration of Biblical Preaching, entitled "A Priest, A Rabbi, and a Lutheran Pastor Walk into a Bar: What Preachers Can Learn from Stand-Up Comedians" (hint: it's not how to be funny). We wish to thank Sally Peters, who invited Karl to present at that conference, and those who attended and offered feedback. This project also had early roots in an article that the two of us published in the journal *Word & World*, entitled "'Everyone Who Hears Will Laugh with Me': Humor and Telling God's Truth."[3] Thank you to the editors of *Word & World*—Fred Gaiser and Mark Granquist—for the invitation to write that piece and the permission to reuse some elements of that essay in this volume. We wish to thank Scott Tunseth and Elvis Ramirez, our faithful and fabulous editors at Fortress Press, for their constant support, encouragement, and great work. We are also grateful to the other members of the Working Preacher Books leadership team—Beth Gaede, Ben McDonald Coltvet, and Karoline Lewis—for the chance to write this book. It means a great deal to us that those who work with us closely, and know us so well, are nevertheless interested in what we might have to say.

Thanks to Will Willimon for writing an apt and generous foreword to this book. Thanks to the Lutheran Church of the Good Shepherd and Luther Seminary for calling us to serve in those settings and graciously allowing us the space to write and speak. And a special thanks to the boys of Sommer Ro: David Lillejord, Hans Wiersma, Mark Tiede, Mike Pancoast, and Tim Martenson. They are dearly beloved friends, deeply respected colleagues, and desperately needed preachers of the gospel of Jesus Christ. We have learned more about ministry from them than we could ever acknowledge. We have laughed together through pain, loss, joy, and new life. We thank God for them. This book is for them. Oh, and for Darrell Kyle as well.

# 1

# A Priest, a Rabbi, and a Pastor Step into a Pulpit

## *Preaching, Humor, and Stand-Up Comedy*

What preachers do is more than a little bit crazy. "The foolishness of our proclamation,"[1] as Paul put it, is quite literally all that we have to offer, and it is a strange enterprise.

> Preachers proclaim forgiveness.
> Preachers dare to speak with the power of God's word and in God's name.
> Preachers speak truth to power.
> Preaching—its task, its goal, the practice of honing it—is a peculiar vocation, almost unique.

We are going to make the assumption that many (if not most, or all) preachers want to improve; they want to grow as orators, hone their craft; they want to be the best that they can be in service of the gospel. And again, most of us preachers have had our various influences: homiletics professors, books about preaching or by great preachers, preachers whom we have heard and seek to emulate. But the time may well come (and perhaps already has for you, dear reader) when one needs to look outside of the discipline itself in order to advance one's practice of it; think of it as interdisciplinary reflection.

So where can the preacher go for help? Who else stands up in front of a room full of people who have nothing in common other than that they are seated facing in the same direction and starts talking to them? While there may well be several options (from sports commentators to news anchors, perhaps even to politicians), we would suggest that the preacher can find no better rhetorical kin than the stand-up comedian.

## Preachers and Stand-Ups

What preachers do is more than a little bit crazy, or, as Chris Rock puts it, *freakish*: "The ability to talk to a lot of people is freakish. It's more freakish than being able to run fast, or dunk a basketball, or any of those other things. It's freakish. Do you think Superman could talk to a thousand people? [To] get their attention . . . he has to bend something first. But to just get up in front of a thousand people and start talking . . ."[2]

Preaching and stand-up have this in common: the challenge of standing in front of a bunch of folks—many of them strangers, or at best acquaintances—and trying to reach them, touch them, and move them, never knowing what you will get from them in response.[3] This is an inherent rhetorical challenge that is shared by preachers and stand-ups, and while preachers are rarely heckled during their preaching (directly), something similar can often happen during the coffee hour or over brunch.

But more than simply sharing a rhetorical challenge, comedians and preachers occupy similar cultural spaces. The culture in which we live and the context in which we practice our wild vocation need our attention in order for our message to come through as authentic and relevant.

In *Preaching at the Crossroads: How the World—and Our Preaching—Is Changing*, David Lose talks about the challenge of preaching:

> If we are called to proclaim good news that is not just old news or the daily news but regularly surprises and even arrests our hearers, then perhaps preachers should not be surprised by the inherent and unending challenge of doing that. . . .
>
> So if the task of fashioning a homiletic appropriate to our age eludes us at present, perhaps that's because we haven't yet sufficiently embraced the mysterious new world in which we live and to which we are called to preach.[4]

And as we have urged, "The church must speak in a fashion that is faithful to Scripture and tradition, but in a register that is fitting to whatever context in which it finds itself—in a way that translates the gospel message into language and symbols that can be understood."[5]

So how might one embrace the mystery—not only of what preaching is but of what preaching is supposed to *do*? We suggest one way is to turn and listen to the art of stand-up comedy, because it *models a different and helpful posture*. The humorous is a register that offers a set of postures with which to perceive the world and speak truth to the world. Observational humor, politically charged material, quick-hitting one-liners, and even "shock" comedy are all part and parcel of the present cultural milieu. Again, from Lose, "Christian theology, at its best, embraces the mystery of the culture in which it finds itself so it can understand, appreciate, and ultimately speak into that mystery in ways that are appropriate and helpful."[6]

Stand-up comedy is—to state the obvious—about humor. Its goal is to evoke laughter. And there are, of course, different kinds of laughter: laughter at something or someone; laughter about something; laughter under or behind; laughter that is joyful; laughter that is bitter, harsh, or sad; laughter that is reactive; and laughter that is invitational. Each of these types of laughter, and the various kinds of humor that may evoke them, may be discernable in the biblical text. So it seems to us that approaching the text and the task of preaching with a hermeneutics of humor in mind can orient the interpreter and the preacher first to the true or full nature of the text, and then to a different way of speaking God's word, one that is "appropriate and helpful" in the present culture.

Further, comedians are, more and more, being taken seriously. The "fake news," as Norm Macdonald called it, which started out on *Saturday Night Live* as "Weekend Update," was social commentary masquerading as a send-up of a news program. This masquerade has become, in a very real sense, a legitimate means of delivering the news. From *The Daily Show* to *The Colbert Report* and now to *Last Week Tonight*, comedic takes on the news have become the primary or only means by which many get their news. Period.

It follows, it seems to us, that while not going so far as to turn preaching into stand-up comedy, we might learn something about the art of preaching from the art of stand-up comedy.

This all began for us as we listened to stand-up comedians. Simply put, we enjoy stand-up and are in the habit of listening in. And it should be no surprise that stand-up comics deal with religion, the religious, and the Bible a great deal. From Sam Kinison's routine about Jesus and the resurrection ("Jesus is the only guy who ever came back from the dead and didn't scare . . . everybody, man"[7]), to Bill Burr's skewering of Christians for his sense of their inconsistency ("Jesus likes hookers and lepers . . . doesn't like queers"[8]), to Jim Gaffigan naming the discomfort that arises when people talk to other people about religion ("Does anything make you feel more uncomfortable than some stranger going, 'I'd like to talk to you about Jesus'?"[9])—and there are, of course, many, many more examples.

Stand-up comedy offers more than entertainment. Stand-up comedians recognize and see clearly topics and their moving parts. Stand-ups often look at the world in particular ways, ways that we preachers will recognize as familiar. As we begin our reflections on stand-up comedy and preaching, and more fully on humor as a theological lens for interpretation in service of preaching, we turn now to three fundamental similarities between stand-up comedy and proclamation: seeing the world askance, the power of intrusion, and the practice of truth telling.

## Seeing the World Askance

In his 2017 special, "Never Grow Up," Bryan Callen made the claim (tongue in cheek, presumably) that while he has only one skill set—being funny—that one skill makes him funnier than all the great men of history. Not *better* than them, but funnier. "Great men," he says, "aren't funny." He continues,

> Even Jesus. . . . No, I don't know, I'm just saying, he was awesome, and he was better and everything. I just don't know how funny he was. . . . I'm sure, walking on water, amazing, but stand-up . . . this takes a long time.[10]

Comedians, as this bit shows, tend to view the world somewhat askew or askance, and that view—a kind of hermeneutical lens for daily life—serves to frame, reframe, and even deframe reality. This can also be a way of looking at the world theologically. Reinhold Niebuhr remarked that "the intimate relation between humour and faith is derived from the fact that both deal with the incongruities of our existence."[11]

We would say, further, that humor and faith share a *wrestling* with and even a *reveling* in the incongruities of life and the "stuff" of faith: the biblical text, the apparent absurdity of faith, and the absurd people who claim to live a faithful life that demands things like loving others as much or more than oneself—which is crazy. Or forgiving your brother (ahem) as many as seventy-seven times, or seventy times seven, which, while surely necessary, seems less than possible. Or selling everything one owns and giving it to the poor in order to ease one's passage through the eye of a needle—which is crazy, *and* less than possible.

The stuff of the life of faith is the stuff of incongruity. Think of those incongruities (!): A dead man has risen from the grave; this man is not just a human being but God as well. The claims about this man's death—*his* death means that *your* sins are forgiven, his *death* means that you have *life*—are laughable. Ask Sarah or Peter, and one out of two thieves on the cross.

Many comedians are funny because they have learned to see and revel in small details in the world—and they've learned to notice what is funny in those details. And then they've figured out how to speak about those details in ways that make people become aware of (and laugh at) those details. Recall (or YouTube) Jerry Seinfeld's famous bit about the missing sock. Or Jim Gaffigan's great bits on Hot Pockets and bacon. Or Mitch Hedberg's hilarious bit about when the family called from a restaurant waiting list ("Dufresne, party of two") doesn't respond, and after calling the name a few times, they move on to the next family: "'Bush, party of three.' Yeah, but what happened to the Dufresnes? No one seems to care! Who can eat at a time like this? People are missing! . . . We need help. Bush, *search* party of three! You can eat once you find the Dufresnes."[12]

In a similar vein, the preacher must learn to see the work of God and the kingdom of God in daily life. And the preacher must then learn to speak about the kingdom of God in ways that make people become aware of the kingdom. Walter Brueggemann has called this skill "prophetic imagination."[13] There is a world in front of us. And the dominant epistemological worldview has taught us not to see either the agency of God or the kingdom of God in that world. Brueggemann writes, "The task of prophetic ministry is to nurture, nourish, and evoke a consciousness and perception alternative to the consciousness and perception of the dominant culture around us."[14] Let those with eyes to see, see.

## The Power of Intrusion, Both Comic and Theological

If the key to comedy is timing, as some have said, then its beating heart is surprise. Cicero talked about "expectation" in comedy; for Descartes, it was "surprise"; for Kant and Hegel, "incongruity." Regardless of the particular term one uses to get at it, a fundamental building block of comedy is the juxtaposition of incongruities. The comedic, at its most basic, is the sudden resolution of a shared expectation into something totally other, or nothing at all. The resolution or transformation of expectation is a different way of perceiving and understanding reality.

The gospel itself is the greatest incongruity in all creation—the reality that the crucifixion and resurrection of the son of God is the moment when God was most present and fully revealed. It is the task of preachers to aid in the gospel's intrusion into our world, to preach in such a way that people are given ears to hear and eyes to see the kingdom, to speak in such a way that it changes the way people see themselves and their neighbors.

As Niebuhr writes, "Humour manages to resolve incongruities by the discovery of another level of congruity."[15] And when that congruity—unexpected and surprising—is discovered, bitter laughter becomes joyful, hopeful laughter.

The most obvious—and the most dealt with—example of this must be the laughter of Sarah, who turns from bitter disbelief to incredulous joy (Gen 18). And it is possible—*likely* even—that one can see in Sarah's story God's reworking of reality and deframing of cultural judgment. Sarah is redeemed from her childlessness and the pregnant burden of cultural shame it carried in the ancient world. God is laughing with and through it all, changing Sarah's laughter from the despair of Friday to the joy of Sunday. Talking about the laughter of Sarah (and of Abraham) in this story, Frederick Buechner concludes,

> Maybe the most interesting part of it all is that far from getting angry at them for laughing, God told them that when the baby was born he wanted them to name him Isaac, which in Hebrew means laughter. So you can say

> that God not only tolerated their laughter but blessed it and in a sense joined in it himself, which makes it a very special laughter indeed—God and man laughing together, sharing a glorious joke in which both of them are involved.[16]

One might say that the one who laughs with God laughs best.

Another example of this is in Paul's familiar hymn at the end of 1 Corinthians. In his ode to the ultimate reframing of reality—of life out of death and this perishable body putting on imperishability—this is the climax:

> Death has been swallowed up in victory.
> Where, O death, is your victory?
> Where, O death, is your sting? (1 Cor 15:54b–55)

What Paul is doing—whether Paul's congregation would have recognized it or not—is borrowing the language of the prophet Hosea:

> Shall I ransom them from the power of Sheol?
>     Shall I redeem them from Death?
> O Death, where are your plagues?
>     O Sheol, where is your destruction? (Hos 13:14)

Paul takes up Hosea's language, turning these phrases into mocking, laughing praise of what God in Christ Jesus does for this frail flesh. Paul's "Where, O death, is your victory? / Where, O death, is your sting?" mocks death's power. And more, it is a reversal of what the prophet intended. Hosea 13:14 ends with the dire conclusion, "Compassion is hidden from my eyes." God, in

Hosea, is speaking judgment against a sinful people. Paul makes of Hosea's words something altogether different, dropping this expected (?) conclusion and instead singing the prophecy as a punch line. We think it reasonable and instructive to see in this theological intrusion and reversal a comic flavor as well.

## Truth Telling

One of the most intrusive parts of human speech is the simple yet often difficult and even dangerous practice of speaking the truth. And stand-up comedians are relentless truth tellers. Most (if not all) comedians practice some sort of truth telling. They are not just telling jokes; they are getting at something deeper. In 2011, HBO aired a special called *Talking Funny*, which was a conversation about comedy among Jerry Seinfeld, Chris Rock, Ricky Gervais, and Louis C. K. Louis C. K. had this to say about the purpose of comedy: "A great thing about comedy is taking people to places that they have fear and foreboding, and making them laugh in that place. I think you help them."[17]

One can think of many examples, but the comedy of *Key & Peele* comes to mind. Keegan-Michael Key and Jordan Peele are two Black comedians. One of the underlying themes their comedy explores is racism and the effects of racism on Black Americans. One of their recurring routines was President Barack Obama's "Anger Translator" named Luther (we kind of love that name!). Peele would play the stoic and decorous President Obama. Key would then play Luther, translating "Obama's" staid speeches into furious tirades.

The task of the preacher is remarkably similar. In fact, it may be identical. Peter Berger puts it this way: "The comic experience provides a distinctive diagnosis of the world. It sees through the facades of ideational and social order, and discloses other realities lurking behind the superficial ones."[18] This is what many comedians do, with more fearlessness and abandon than many preachers dare.

We preachers could do worse than to learn from their example, because this is precisely what God's word, and the preacher of that word, does. The task of the preacher is to tell the truth, to expose sin and death, to proclaim law and gospel, to preach Christ and him crucified to a world that too often does not know him. Furthermore, and profoundly important, this is, according to Martin Luther, what defines the theologian of the cross: "A theologian of the cross calls the thing what it actually is."[19] A theologian of the cross must tell the truth—calling a thing what it actually is. Sin is sin. Death is death. Love is love. Forgiveness brings new life.

## The Foolishness of Our Proclamation

One objection that may be made to this whole idea of putting the stand-up comedian and the preacher in conversation with each other is that comedians are often seen as modern-day court jesters. They are irreverent, clownish, and contrary. In other words, offensive. But as Berger tells us, "One of the important social functions of humor seems always to have been to outrage conventional moral sentiments."[20]

As preachers engage with comedians, there will be (at least) two ways in which this is troubling and true. First is the nature of our proclamation itself. If the Bible is to be believed, proclamation saves people by naming the salvation of the triune God as having come near. Through preaching, the triune God's salvation breaks into the "now" and creates the faith that receives that salvation as good news. Preaching and listening, empowered by the work of the Spirit, bring people to faith. As Paul put it to the Romans, "Faith comes from what is heard, and what is heard comes through the word of Christ" (Rom 10:17). This is, it seems, how God chooses to operate—through words. Quite literally from the beginning, this has been God's approach. But as the Bible itself tells us, this preaching to faith is best understood as a kind of foolishness, at least to some. The idea that preaching is a means of grace and the primary medium of faith formation is troubling indeed and will outrage some, if not many.

Second is the response that we can expect, at least in part, to this foolishness that we proclaim. To quote Berger once more, "What to faith is the most real (*ens realissimum*) is to the nonbelieving mind a fantasy; conversely, the hard reality of a mundane worldview is, in the eyes of faith, a fleeting fantasy."[21]

The message about the cross *is* foolishness, as Paul himself acknowledged:

> For the message about the cross is foolishness to those who are perishing, but to us who are being saved it is the power of God. For it is written,
>
> "I will destroy the wisdom of the wise,
> and the discernment of the discerning I will thwart."
>
> . . . For since, in the wisdom of God, the world did not know God through wisdom, God decided, through the foolishness of our proclamation, to save those who believe. For Jews demand signs and Greeks desire wisdom, but we proclaim Christ crucified, a stumbling block to Jews

> and foolishness to Gentiles, but to those who are the called, both Jews and Greeks, Christ the power of God and the wisdom of God. For God's foolishness is wiser than human wisdom, and God's weakness is stronger than human strength. (1 Cor 1:18–19, 21–25)

The word of the cross is outrageous, and at times outraging. And in the midst of this outrageousness stands the preacher. He or she and you and we are, apparently, fools. Or to be even more aggressive, morons, which is what the Greek word Paul uses for "foolishness" means when it is used as a personal noun. Not to put too fine a point on it, you who are reading this are, in a very real way, a moron. But you are *God's* moron, God's jester, God's fool.

The old adage says, "The fool speaks truth to power." Like the stand-up, this is the preacher's vocation as well—to speak the gospel truth to power, to the "powers that be," the powers of this world, the powers that rule in peoples' lives. And humor in reading Scripture, in interpreting the biblical text for the practice of preaching, in all of its askanceness and intrusion, is just what such truth telling needs. This may cause outrage, but it is what we preachers are meant for, because "the reality is that humor is tremendously effective at exposing the not-so-pleasant realities of life in a broken world."[22] Or, as Helmut Thielicke puts it, "If comedy were given a place in theology, it would be in the realm of eschatology. I.e., in the laughter of the faithful, God's future breaks into the now."[23]

So is the preacher the court jester of the church? The fool? Maybe so and maybe that is a good thing. Recall the recurring role that the fool plays in Shakespeare's plays: the fool is present not merely for comic relief but to tell the truth. One thinks of

Feste in *Twelfth Night*, the clown in *Othello*, Falstaff in several plays, the fool in *King Lear*, and the rest of Shakespeare's clowns, jesters, and fools. The fool speaks a vital truth that the other characters usually cannot perceive. And while the characters in the play do not always understand the truth that the fool speaks, the audience does. In *Twelfth Night*, Feste shows superior discernment and intelligence. "Better a witty fool than a foolish wit," he says. But he also says, "I wear not motley in my brain."[24] As Isaac Asimov famously wrote in his *Guide to Shakespeare*, "That, of course, is the great secret of the successful fool—that he is no fool at all."[25] And of course, the preacher is no fool. Some of us, after all, have fancy titles before our names and initialed letters after. We cannot truly be fools, can we? Well, better a preaching fool than a foolish preacher.

One last word: if there is truth to another old adage that "laughter is the best medicine," perhaps it may also be said that "laughter is the best theology." And this is the theological conversation to which we are inviting you.

# 2

# "I Don't Care Who You Are; That's Funny Right There"

## *Letting the Bible Be Funny*

A common impression about religion and the Bible is that there is no humor to be found. To quote Bryan Callen, "I've been to church, I've read the Bible, never laughed once."[1] In many ways, it seems to us, religion is often a stuffy business. Religion deals with serious issues, of course: matters of life and death, of sin and its consequences, of justice, of pain and fear and hurt—serious business. And so there seems to be an assumption that we need always to be serious about it, even grim. In some ways, it seems that "the church" has often taken Ecclesiastes 7:6 to heart:

> For like the crackling of thorns under a pot,
> so is the laughter of fools; this also is vanity.

Or, perhaps, Sirach 27:13:

The talk of fools is offensive,
and their laughter is wantonly sinful.

Indeed, the sixth-century "Rule of Benedict" (which has been among the most influential documents in the history of the Western Christian tradition) states, "Do not speak words that are idle or suited to laughter." And also, "Buffoonery or words which are useless and provoke laughter—these we condemn with a perpetual ban, and the disciple is not permitted to open his mouth for such conversation."

But the Bible is often funny, both intentionally and unintentionally, and if we are to be true to the text and open the Bible more fully (and faithfully), we need to let the Bible be funny when it is funny, because it will be more meaningful if we can let its humor breathe.

Take, for example, the story of Isaac, Rebekah, and Abimelech, the king of the Philistines, in Genesis 26. In this scene, Isaac pulls the "she's my sister" trick his father, Abraham, had taught him (cf. Gen 12 and 20). There was a famine in the land, so Isaac and Rebekah went to the land of the Philistines where there was food. When the "men of the place" asked about Rebekah—who was easy on the eyes—Isaac said, "She's my sister," because he was afraid they might kill him and take Rebekah. In and of itself, this story is another of the trickster-themed stories that are the recurring stuff of the ancestral narratives. These stories would surely have inspired laughter and glee as tricks are played on the more powerful and the less faithful. But there is a twist in this story that is funnier still.

In Genesis 26:8–9a we read, "When Isaac had been there a long time, King Abimelech of the Philistines looked out of a window and saw him fondling his wife Rebekah. So Abimelech called for Isaac, and said, 'So she is your wife!'" The key phrase here is Abimelech "saw [Isaac] fondling his wife Rebekah." In Hebrew that phrase is יִצְחָק מְצַחֵק אֵת רִבְקָה (*yitschaq metsachēq 'et ribqāh*). The NRSV translates the verb as "fondling," the NJPS as "sporting," and the NIV as "caressing." All these translations are, frankly, safe ways of dodging the obvious—and examples of flubbing the punch line. The translation of the ESV comes a little closer to getting it right: Abimelech "saw Isaac laughing with Rebekah his wife"—translating מְצַחֵק as "laughing." This is close, but in some ways, it is the most wrong, since it renders מְצַחֵק (*metsachēq*) too literally, missing the joke.

We will let the always hilarious *The Hebrew and Aramaic Lexicon of the Old Testament* make the joke.[2] It translates the verb here as "dally with, fondle." Seriously, "dally"? Who uses that word in daily life? Nobody! The scene presents us with Isaac and Rebekah engaging in something far more intimate than laughing together, or even engaging in a casual "public display of affection"—otherwise, why would it have tipped off Abimelech that the two were married? This is a case in which the play on words will almost always be lost in translation, and the humor of the story with it. If we translate יִצְחָק מְצַחֵק אֵת רִבְקָה (*yitschaq metsachēq 'et ribqāh*) quite literally, we will see what Abimelech sees as he looks out the window: Abimelech "saw Isaac *isaacing* Rebekah his wife." The whole thing is funny, because it is a play on Isaac's name—the Hebrew verb *tsāchaq* means "laugh," but it is also a euphemism for having sex. Isaac and Rebekah were doing what lovebirds do. They were having sex. If this story were set in a modern sitcom, as Abimelech looked out the window and saw Isaac and Rebekah getting it on, the soundtrack we would hear is the opening of Barry White's "Never, Never Gonna Give Ya Up" ("Oh baby, my baby, keep on doing it . . . right on . . .").

And that's funny. It's beautiful, touching, lovely, and hilarious.

Then there is the story of Elijah and the prophets of Baal. At the climax of the contest, Elijah turns to mockery of Baal and his prophets, saying, "Cry aloud! Surely he is a god; either he is meditating, or he has wandered away, or he is on a journey, or perhaps he is asleep and must be awakened" (1 Kgs 18:27). The Hebrew verb translated here as "wandered away" most likely means—we will once again quote that great comic handbook, *The Hebrew and Aramaic Lexicon of the Old Testament*—"expulsion, defecation." To translate the whole thing more accurately, "Surely [Baal] is god! Either he's praying to himself, or having himself a good bowel movement, or maybe he's on vacation. Perhaps he's napping and needs to be awakened." Elijah digs and keeps digging, making theological mock of the "god" who does not answer. This is trash-talking, and it is meant to illicit laughter.

Or how about Elisha, with the snotty little kids and the she-bears? It is a story that almost seems thrown in and is certainly something of a non sequitur. While traveling from Jericho to Mount Carmel, Elijah passes by Bethel, where he is the victim of trash-talking as a pack of feral youth make fun of him: "Hey, Baldy! Get lost!" Elisha's response? He curses them, and they are attacked by she-bears. That's what you get for mocking a prophet of the Lord. Now, to be fair, this is a little much, and the modern reader may well find this story hard to take. But while this reads more like an episode from *Grimm's Fairy Tales*, it is actually a strange sort of miracle, and we think it safe to assume that while the point of it may be to demonstrate Elisha's power and authority as a prophet (he has just inherited Elijah's mantle earlier in the chapter), the way it demonstrates his power was meant to be humorous.

In a different way, the whole book of Jonah is humorous. Everything is "big," extreme, and even ridiculous. The story has something of the farce about it. There is the big city, the big wind, the big storm, the big fish, and so on (גָּדוֹל, "big" or "great" in Hebrew, is used fourteen times in Jonah). There is Jonah's confession of faith in God made even while he is running away from God's calling. There is the brevity of his sermon delivered to the Ninevites when he finally does answer God's call (just five words long in Hebrew), and there is the over-the-top repentance that comes in response to it, with every living thing in Nineveh putting on sackcloth and fasting. There is a silliness and a sham seriousness to the story that is arresting and inviting. But the questions of whether or not Nineveh was actually as large as a three-days walk across and if Jonah really was inside the belly of a whale for three days and three nights are not really the point. What matters is how funnily the story is laid out and the irony that lurks in every scene.

Or take the book of Daniel. (No really, take it.)

Take the hilarious story of King Nebuchadnezzar and the fiery furnace. If you let this tale breathe, you will realize how funny it is. In some congregations, this story is read at the annual Easter Vigil worship service—which is a somber and . . . um . . . really long worship service on the Saturday between Good Friday and Easter Sunday. Maybe this solemn worship setting is what prevents so many people from understanding the humor in the story. In the story, all the details are hyperbolic and satirical. King Nebuchadnezzar is a bit of a buffoon. He erects a golden statue of absurd proportions: "ninety feet high and nine feet thick" (MSG). He gathers "the satraps, the prefects, and the governors, the counselors, the treasurers, the justices, the magistrates, and *allllllllll* the officials of the provinces" (our emphasis). He then orders "all the satraps, the prefects, and the governors, the counselors, the treasurers, the justices, the magistrates, and *allllllllll* the officials of the provinces" (our emphasis; the repetition is part of the humor), "When you hear the sound of the horn, pipe, lyre, trigon, harp, drum, and entire musical ensemble, you are to fall down and worship the golden statue that King Nebuchadnezzar has set up. Whoever does not fall down and worship shall immediately be thrown into a furnace of blazing fire" (Dan 3:5–7). Shadrach, Meshach, and Abednego—three Jewish boys who take the first commandment seriously—refuse to comply with this absurd decree.

Some snitches turn them in: "O King, may you live forever! You, O King, have made a decree that whenever anyone hears the sound of the horn, pipe, lyre, trigon, harp, drum, or any kind of music, they are to fall down and worship the golden statue. . . . But Shadrach, Meshach, and Abednego, these boys pay you no heed, O King. They do not serve your gods and they do not worship the golden statue that you erected!" (Dan 3:10–12; our translation). And on it goes. The narrative uses the repetition of the farcically long lists and the hyperbole of the huge golden statue and overly hot furnace to mock the empire and bring the audience to laughter. In this way, it stands up to the violence and hostility that exilic and postexilic Jews so often experienced from the empire. Because, as we all know, humor is one of the few weapons with which powerless people are armed in the face of empire. And humor is one of the few things that emperors seem to fear.

And lest one think that only the Old Testament is funny, we can find humor in the New as well. Read Mark 9:14–29, the story of a child with an unclean spirit. The child is brought to Jesus, and the child's father asks Jesus to heal the boy, "if you are able" (9:23). Jesus responds with what sounds like a little indignation: "*If* you are able!" (9:24). It is as if Jesus says, "YOU brought him to ME, and now say IF. . . . All things can be done for one who believes." And the boy's father, an ancient forerunner of Yogi Berra, utters one of the great contradictions of all time: "I believe; help my unbelief!" Which is it? It is an incongruous and absurd statement he makes, and yet in that absurdity is the truth of faith, which is often comingled with doubt.

Another example of a story that may be freshly read with an eye to humor is the wedding at Cana (John 2:1–12). First, there is the strangeness of the setting, with the Christ called by his mom to make sure that the party keeps going. The wine is gone, and Jesus can fix that. When he objects, "My hour has not yet come" (John 2:4), his mother Mary pulls a classic mom move and ignores him, turning to the caterers and saying, "Do whatever he tells you" (John 2:5). Presumably reluctantly, Jesus gets to work, and unlike when our children do as they are told without any real interest in doing what they've been told, Jesus performs marvelously, making wine that is better than the good wine first served. And as one preacher said about this text during a wedding sermon in a church that only allowed one champagne toast during wedding receptions, "Jesus didn't give them just a little wine, enough for one champagne toast. No, Jesus gave them six huge vats of the best wine ever—enough to get the entire wedding party into serious trouble!" And, we are told, "his disciples believed in him" (John 2:11). Who wouldn't? We'd RSVP for that wedding!

Or how about the call of Nathanael? When Philip tells Nathanael that they have found the promised messiah, "Jesus, son of Joseph from Nazareth," Nathanael replies sardonically or sarcastically, "Can anything good come out of Nazareth?" (John 1:45–46).

Two more. Consider Isaiah 56:3–5. There is an exquisite wordplay going on in these verses, with a morbidly funny reimagination of inclusion. In Isaiah 56, there is some back-and-forth language regarding being joined to and/or separated from the Lord and his community. Recall that the "sign" of inclusion in the Abrahamic covenant is male circumcision (see Gen 17:10–14). For this reason, foreigners who did not wish to be circumcised and eunuchs—who could not be circumcised—were traditionally excluded from the covenant. In Isaiah 56:3–8, which is Third Isaiah's inaugural message, the prophet welcomes both foreigners and eunuchs into the covenant. The prophet uses the imagery of the eunuch as a "dry tree"—which, to be clear, is a blatantly phallic reference to castration. What Third Isaiah is doing by using this kind of language is deframing the prohibitions of Deuteronomy 23, and doing so glibly. All of which can, again, be lost in translation—in one case literally. Eugene Peterson, in his beautiful paraphrase of the Hebrew Bible, gets at the *heart* of what Isaiah is up to in these verses exactly right, on the one hand, while one the other hand, he clearly misses the *humor* of the text. Compare the following (our emphasis):

NRSV

Do not let the foreigner *joined* to the Lord say,
"The Lord will surely *separate* me from his people";
and do not let the eunuch say,
"*I am just a dry tree.*"

4 For thus says the Lord:
To the eunuchs who keep my sabbaths,
who choose the things that please me
and hold fast my covenant,
5 I will give, in my house and within my walls,
a monument and a name
better than sons and daughters;
I will give them an everlasting name
that *shall not be cut off.*

## The Message

"Make sure no outsider who now follows God
ever has occasion to say, '*God put me in
second-class.*
*I don't really belong.*'
And make sure no physically mutilated person is ever
made to think,
'*I'm damaged goods.*
*I don't really belong.*'"
4–5 For God says:
"To the mutilated who keep my Sabbaths
and choose what delights me
and keep a firm grip on my covenant,
I'll provide them an honored place
in my family and within my city,
even more honored than that of sons and
daughters.
I'll confer permanent honors on them
*that will never be revoked.*"

This is an amazing word of grace and inclusion that Isaiah could simply have declared. But he is clearly having fun while he is doing it. Consider the words *joined, separated, dry tree, cut off, mutilated*—all about the eunuch! Isaiah takes a dark and difficult reality; being made by the empire into a eunuch was a terrible experience. It was done to men, usually young men who were slaves or illegitimate sons of a king or official. Eunuchs by definition could not have children, which meant in the ancient imagination that they also could not have a heritage; they would not pass on their name to future generations. And in the case of the religion of ancient Israel, this also meant that one was necessarily excluded from worship and the life of the community.

But here, Isaiah reports that God was doing a new thing. God was gathering in the outcasts. God was transforming the suffering and shame of those who had been made eunuchs through no choice of their own; conferring upon them honor, love, laughter; and declaring to them, in Peterson's translation, "I'll provide them an honored place in my family and within my city, even more honored than that of sons and daughters." God was laughing an Easter laugh with those who had been "cut off" from the covenant people, offering them a joyful community and new hope and life.

And then there is Galatians 5, where Paul goes wild with the circumcision bit, taking it to the next level in what sounds to us like smack talk:

> But my friends, why am I still being persecuted if I am still preaching circumcision? In that case the offense of the cross has been removed. I wish those who unsettle you would castrate themselves! (5:11–12)

Go Paul.

In each of these cases, while we would not necessarily go so far as to say that one *has* to see the humor in order to understand them, seeing the humor can open the texts up differently and more fully.

## Bringing Humor to the Text

Another old truism about comedy is that some people say funny things, while other people say things funny (in an amusing manner). This truism resonates with our sense of the biblical text as well. Some stories seem to be intentionally humorous, while others can come across as funny. In the latter case, it seems to us that we can bring humor to the text in such a way that while the text may not have been intended to be humorous, it may still have that effect, or may be fruitfully informed by levity. Bringing humor to the text may function in at least a couple of ways.

First, it can be an incidental, almost accidental reaction to the text—reflexive amusement when our spiritual funny bone is struck. For example, we often find the book of Proverbs hilarious. We cannot prove that any of those proverbial bits of wisdom were set to scroll with a snicker in the corner of the scribe's mouth, but consider the following:

> Like a dog that returns to its vomit is a fool who reverts to his folly. (Prov 26:11)

> As a door turns on its hinges, so does a lazy person in bed. (Prov 26:14)

> It is better to live in a corner of the housetop than in a house shared with a contentious wife. (Prov 21:9)

> It is better to live in a desert land than with a contentious and fretful wife. (Prov 21:19)

> A continual dripping on a rainy day and a contentious wife are alike. (Prov 27:15)

Seems like the editor of the book of Proverbs was not happily married; and to be fair, these would be good verses to translate in an inclusive way as, say, "a contentious *spouse*." After all, more than a few wives have been married to contentious men. Still, these verses aim at telling the truth and are funny at the same time. In fact, we think that the humor of these proverbs is what makes them memorable.

Second, bringing humor to the text can be, in a sense, an artificial lens that we hold over it. In some ways this is what most comedians do when they practice their art on the biblical text. Jim Gaffigan has a routine where he is talking about Moses and his call. When the people ask Moses what happened, he says that God spoke to him as a burning bush: "Sure he did. Moses, we think maybe you've been burning some 'bush.'"[3]

It is the play on words that drives the joke. Then again there is a recent special by Jerry Seinfeld in which he compares the moment when the Pop-Tart was first unveiled (when all we had was toast) to Moses's bringing forth the Ten Commandments.

Martin Luther sometimes read the Bible in a similar way, applying the story of Balaam and his mule to his own life, saying, "If God then spoke through the mouth of an ass against a prophet, why should he not be able even now to speak through a righteous man?"[4] One of our seminary professors, Mark Throntveit, often did the same. As we were reading and translating the story of Elijah and the Shunammite woman in 2 Kings 4, we arrived at verse 27: "When she came to the man of God at the mountain, she caught hold of his feet." We had been talking about how in Hebrew, euphemisms are frequent. One such is the frequent use of "feet" as a euphemism for "genitals." But in this case, Throntveit said, "Sometimes a foot is just a foot."

Third, we can bring humor to texts that are not explicitly humorous by the way that we read them—that is, *the way we read them out loud, the way we perform the texts.* One of our friends is a hilarious woman who reads the biblical text with such drama and humor that one cannot help but laugh. We recall her way of reading Amos 4:1:

> Hear this word, you cows of Bashan
>     who are on Mount Samaria,
> Who oppress the poor, who crush the needy,
>     who say to their husbands, "Bring something to
>         drink!"

As she reads the passage aloud, she first adopts a humorously scolding tone—the tone of one who is upbraiding a persistently disobedient loved one: "Oh you cows of Bashan . . ." But just after she reads "who say to their husbands," she leans back in her chair, flings out her right arm, and then—in her very best bored-but-entitled, wealthy suburban woman voice—says, "Bring me a drink!" And notice the way the joke is almost just waiting there in the text (almost, we say).

Many jokes contain three elements—a priest, a rabbi, and a pastor; a Norwegian, a German, and a Swiss; a baseball player, a basketball player, and a soccer player; and so on. In most jokes, the first two elements set the pattern, and then the third element breaks the pattern in a surprising and funny way. In Amos 4:1, the prophet is naming the dire sins of the wealthy women of Samaria. They are people (1) "who oppress the poor," (2) "who crush the needy," and (3) . . . we are waiting for something like "who exploit widows and orphans," but we get "who say to their husbands, 'Bring something to drink!'" We doubt Amos was telling a standard three-element joke, but darn, after hearing our friend read Amos 4:1, it sure made us laugh.

Another example of this is the parable of the so-called prodigal son (Luke 15:11–32). Our teacher Don Juel used to call this story the "lament of the responsible older child." He used to say that if you have been told that you are just like the younger son, you've probably been brainwashed. If you are a preacher, that is probably very much the case—you are probably much more like the older child in the parable. Don would say that the only interesting character in the parable is the older son. Our retelling of the parable is inspired by Don.[5] We'll join the parable midway through, when the older son—let's pick a random name for him . . . how about Rolf—returns from working in the field.

> Now his older son was in the field working, which is where responsible sons are supposed to be; and when he came and approached the house, he heard music and dancing. He called one of the farmhands over and asked, "What the hell is going on? I hear music. And dancing." And the farmhand said, "Oh, haven't you heard? Your younger brother, Karl [another randomly selected name], has returned. Your dad gave him a

> robe—the best one—some Birkenstocks, and his gold ring. Your dad slaughtered the fatted calf because he got your brother back."
>
> "Wait, the fatted calf? My 4-H calf, the one that I used to feed from a bottle when it was a baby?"
>
> "Yeah, that's the one."
>
> "Why didn't anyone come and get me?"
>
> "I asked if I should go get you, but they said, 'Nah, he's in the field working. He doesn't even like parties—he likes to work.'"
>
> The older brother was so enraged that he refused to join the party. So his father ducked out of the party and begged him to come in. But before his dad could even finish, he interrupted and shouted, "Listen! For all these years I have been working for you like a slave. I never disobeyed even one of your rules. And you never even once gave me a lousy goat so that I might have a party with my friends. But when this son of yours came back—who's wasted your wealth on hookers and heaven knows what else—you killed my fatted calf for him!" [An aside: How did the older son know his brother had partied with prostitutes? Did the kid send postcards? Did he post it on Instagram? TikTok?]
>
> But his father shook his head, "Son, you have always been with me. Everything that is mine is yours. But we had to celebrate. He's still your brother. He was dead, but now he lives. He was lost, but now he's found."

A few years back when we were working through this parable with some college students, at this point in the story, the class laughed.

But one student who was sitting in the front row (where all responsible older children sit) just stared down and through gritted teeth said, "This. Makes. Me. So. MAD! It's not fair." Exactly. By using a little humor to let the parable breathe, the story did its job. Like the fuming-mad Jonah, the student realized that the love of the father isn't fair. God's grace isn't fair. As one of our friends who is a cop says, "The fair's in August. It's where they judge pigs."

The parables of Jesus are wonderful stories to let a little humor in. Even though we often read them as flat, religious truisms that Jesus used in order *not* to get his point across. That in and of itself is kind of funny. But Frederick Buechner has suggested that the parables themselves are actually a kind of joke:

> The kind of joke Jesus told when he said it is harder for a rich person to enter Paradise than for a Mercedes to get through a revolving door. . . . And then added that though for man it is impossible, for God all things are possible because God is the master of the impossible . . . he is in the end a wild and impossible God.[6]

Through this lens, the point of the parables seems to be to surprise, to disorient, and to reframe the way one thinks and believes and behaves. Both the delivery and the impact or reception may be humorous. (More on the parables as jokes follows in chapter 3.)

To draw from Buechner once more, laughter comes from "as deep a place as tears," and as such, it has power: "As much as tears do, [laughter] comes out of the darkness of the world where God is of all missing persons the most missed, except it comes not as an ally of the darkness but as its adversary, not as a symptom of darkness but as its antidote."[7] Humor that moves in, with, and under life's trials can be redemptive.

We began this chapter by saying that the Bible is often funny and that we ought to let it be, to read it as it is and for what it is. In our interpretive tradition, we often talk not about the "literal" meaning of the text but about the "plain" meaning. The plain meaning is both about simply *what* the text says and about *how* the text creates meaning.

The old saying that "familiarity breeds contempt" has a parallel in the question of biblical fluency, and it goes like this: "familiarity breeds complacency." The Bible is a storehouse of surprise if we are reading it for what it is and what it means. The problem is that even with stories that we think we already know, we have not often let certain texts or stories have free rein to be what they actually are. Humor, and the laughter it brings, jars us out of our assumed familiarity, or bubbles forth as we are jarred by what the Bible says, and says plainly.

Think about the Noah story. As an exercise, retell yourself the story. How does it end? Most of us, even if we are very familiar with the biblical narrative, will say that it ends with the dove and the olive branch, a rainbow in the heavens, and a little worship. That is what we remember, because that is the Sunday school version of the story. But it does not really end there. The fuller ending of the story involves Noah planting a vineyard, harvesting the grapes, fermenting them, drinking them, stripping naked, and passing out "hammered drunk." His sons then cover him up, and when he wakes up, hungover no doubt, he takes out his shame on his son and kicks him out of the family. To be sure, this is not the stuff of Sunday school, nor of Noah's ark mobiles hanging over infants' cribs. And, equally sure, this is a tragic story, telling the truth about a family's dysfunction. But it is also ironic, ironic that this is the ending of the story of the one righteous man among all humankind. Righteous. Right.

The Bible is frequently funny. Not always "ha-ha" funny, but funny in all sorts of ways. And if we let it be what it is, if we let its humor breathe, the Bible will "mean" more clearly, and be more accessible. What is more, if we let the Bible be what it is, we are actually being more faithful "stewards of the mysteries of God," and our preaching will follow.

# 3

# "No One's Laughing at God; We're All Laughing with God"

## *Theology and a God Who Laughs*

What is your favorite picture of God? When you think of all the biblical images of God, what is your favorite? What portrait captures your theological imagination or tickles your spiritual fancy? Like Saint Peter, do you like the transfigured Jesus best? The Glorious One, up there on the mountain with Moses and Elijah, lit up like the Vegas Strip? Or, like Luther and Paul, those theologians of the cross, do you prefer your God tortured and dead, nailed to the tree? Or, like the great theologian Ricky Bobby of Talladega, do you like the Christmas Jesus best? That eight-pound, six-ounce baby in a fleece diaper—can't talk yet but still omnipotent?

What about a laughing God?

That was one of our mother's favorites. Once, while watching a pair of pileated woodpeckers engaged in their beautifully awkward aerial mating dance, she observed, "The Lord has a strange sense of humor. This must make him laugh." And then she chuckled, much like she thought her Lord would.

But *does* God laugh? Did Jesus *ever laugh*? *Can* the Holy Spirit? Have you ever wondered? A cursory (and even a relatively close) reading of the Bible often leaves the impression that if God does laugh, such laughter is either rare or hidden behind the divine hand. And so Reinhold Niebuhr began his sermon titled "Humour and Faith" like this: "'He that sitteth in the heavens shall laugh: the Lord shall have them in derision' Ps 2:4. This word of the Second Psalm is the only instance in the Bible in which laughter is attributed to God. God is not frequently thought of as possessing a sense of humour."[1]

In one regard, Niebuhr is mistaken, as Psalm 2 is not the only reference to God laughing (more on that in the next section), but in another, he is certainly correct: "There are critics of religion who regard it as deficient in the sense of humour, and they can point to the fact that there is little laughter in the Bible."[2] As we have already said, we believe this is in part because we have wound up with too much church in our Bible and theology, or at least too much of a certain kind of church—the one with pews full of the grim, serious, humorless, faithful.

We will point to a number of places in which God laughs explicitly and, as we will argue, to places where God's laughter is implicit as well.

## God's Laughter in the Old Testament

As Niebuhr noted, God laughs in Psalm 2:4–6, where we read,

> He who sits in the heavens laughs;
> the Lord has them in derision.

Then he will speak to them in his wrath,
and terrify them in his fury, saying,
"I have set my king on Zion, my holy hill."

God's laughter here has a particular tone. One of the fundamental elements of Hebrew poetry is called parallelism. Parallelism is the repetition or echoing of a word or concept within or between lines of poetry. Notice here that "laughs" (שחק/*śāchaq*) is echoed by "derision." Derision in Hebrew is from the root לעג (*lā'ag*) and is its own kind of mocking laughter.[3] God's dismissive laughter is directed at the nations and their leaders who "plot" and "take counsel" against God's own chosen king and people. God is amused by their plotting, but not with a gentle or kindly amusement; rather, it is laughter filled with wrath and fury (Ps 2:5) meant, like the growling of a lion, as a warning (Ps 2:10). In case this turns you off, remember that when human dictators and rulers plot, their plans are often written in blood—wars are waged, battles are born, innocents are killed. The authors of the New Testament read Psalm 2 and couldn't help but think of Jesus: "The kings of the earth [King Herod] . . . and the rulers [Pontius Pilate] take counsel together, against the Lord and his anointed" (Ps 2:2). And what happened? Jesus was nailed to a tree and left there until he died. But God laughs at their plans. Why? Because God raises the dead. Sort of makes this modern proverb sound a little different: While we make our plans, God laughs.

At the end of Psalm 2, after warning that it is foolish to make plans against God and God's Messiah, the psalm culminates with a striking promise that comes as a result of God's dismissive laughter: "Happy are all who take refuge in [God]" (Ps 2:12). "Happy," translated other times as "blessed," may sound different in this case. "Happy" may mean laughing along with God at the foolishness of those who would dare to plot against God and God's people.

Something similar takes place in Psalm 59. The first seven verses are a prayer for deliverance placed in the mouth of David, according to the psalm's superscription, when Saul had his house staked out in order to kill him. The prayer for help expresses its trust in verse 8:

> But you laugh at them, O Lord;
> you hold all the nations in derision. (Ps 59:8)

"Them" again refers to the nations who speak out and "treacherously plot evil" against God's people (Ps 59:5). And as in Psalm 2, again "laughter" and "derision" are in parallel. The psalm describes God's enemies as "bellowing with their mouths, with sharp words on their lips—for 'Who,' they think, 'will hear us?'" (Ps 59:7). "Umm," says the psalmist, "God hears. *You hear*, O God." When the evildoers of the world hatch plots behind closed doors against God's people, it is comforting to know that God hears their planning and just laughs.

Lastly—again from one of the psalms, Psalm 37—God laughs at the wicked because God knows that the time is coming when they will get theirs:

> The wicked plot against the righteous,
> and gnash their teeth at them;
> but the Lord laughs at the wicked,
> for he sees that their day is coming. (37:12–13)

Echoing what we saw in Psalms 2 and 59, when the wicked plot evil against God's people, God dismissively laughs off their petty plans. But what is more, in this case the psalm envisions a day when the wicked will get caught in the very traps that they lay for the righteous because they will be "hoisted with their own petard," as it were:

> The wicked draw the sword and bend their bows
> to bring down the poor and needy,
> to kill those who walk uprightly;
> their sword shall enter their own heart,
> and their bows shall be broken.[4] (Ps 37:14–15)

When that day comes, we can envision the righteous laughing along with God, "for the Lord loves justice; he will not forsake his faithful ones" (Ps 37:28).

The case of Psalm 104 is different. For this poet, the answer to the question we asked at the beginning of this chapter, "What is your favorite picture of God?" might have been "I like to picture the Lord as a child in a bathtub, splashing, playing with some toy boats and a rubber shark, blowing bubbles under the water." Here is why.

In the middle of Psalm 104—a long psalm that praises God as Creator, the sustainer and re-creator of life—the psalmist offers a line that is almost always mistranslated. The New Revised Standard Version has it this way:

> O Lord, how manifold are your works!
> In wisdom you have made them all;
> the earth is full of your creatures.
> Yonder is the sea, great and wide,
> creeping things innumerable are there,
> living things both small and great.

> There go the ships,
>     and Leviathan that you formed to sport in it.
>         (Ps 104:24–26)

The problem is with that last phrase: "Leviathan that you formed to sport in it." The Hebrew phrase is slightly ambiguous. Most commonly, the subject of the verb "sport" is taken to be Leviathan—the sea monster—and the antecedent (remember to thank your high school German teacher Herr Rockey for teaching you what an antecedent is) of "it" is taken as "the sea." And thus, "You formed him [Leviathan] to sport in it [the sea]." But this is an incorrect reading, as a passage in Job establishes. The subject of the verb translated here as "sport" is actually God, and the antecedent of "it" is actually Leviathan. The proper translation is "and Leviathan, the one you made in order to laugh at him." The same subject and verb occur in Job 41:5 in an almost identical construction—and there the meaning is crystal clear. God asks Job if he thinks he can handle Leviathan:

> Can you draw out Leviathan with a fishhook,
>     or press down its tongue with a cord?
> Can you put a rope in its nose,
>     or pierce its jaw with a hook?
> Will it make many supplications to you?
>     Will it speak soft words to you?
> Will it make a covenant with you
>     to be taken as your servant forever?
> *Will you play with it* as with a bird,
>     or will you put it on leash for your girls?
>         (Job 41:1–5)

Will you *play* with him? It should also be noted that this notion of having "fun," of play, is rooted in laughter—the word translated as "sport" in Psalm 104:26 and as "play" in Job 41:5 is the word we've been tracking for over two chapters in this book: שחק/*śāchaq*, "laugh/laughter."[5] The most literal translation of the phrase would be either "Leviathan, whom you formed to laugh at him" or "Leviathan, whom you formed to play with him." This is why we think this phrase in Psalm 104 should be something like one of these: "Leviathan, whom you formed so that you could enjoy him" or "to have fun with him" or "for the fun of it" or simply "to laugh at him." We learned from Jon Levenson to think of Leviathan here as "God's rubber ducky."[6] In the ancient imagination, Leviathan was the chaos monster—the big, scary creature whose abode was the sea, lurking in the depths: "There is terror all around its teeth. Its back is made of shields in rows" (Job 41:14–15).

But there's nothing to be afraid of, says the poet of Psalm 104. Leviathan, a scary monster? Nah, just God's bath toy! And that's how we got the picture of the Lord as a child in a bathtub, playing with toy boats and a rubber ducky. Here is our translation:

> O Lord, how numerous are your creations!
> With wisdom you made them all;
> Indeed, the earth is filled with your creatures.
> Over there is the sea, so great and wide:
> There are tiny things too many to count,
> living things both small and large.
> There are ships that sail back-and-forth,
> and Leviathan, whom you formed to laugh at him.
> (104:24–26)

Like pileated woodpeckers, like narwhals, and like platypuses, Leviathan is laughable. Laughable in a "God saw that it was good" sort of way. God laughs because of Leviathan, in a sheer, delightful, joyful, splashing-in-the-tub kind of way. And if God takes delight in Leviathan the chaos monster, just think how much delight and joy God takes in you—who were literally created in God's image.

But as funny as the image is—of God playing with the great sea monster and laughing all the while—we should not miss its intense, polemical edge. In the ancient Near East, the sea was the place of chaos, in permanent rebellion against the Lord and the Lord's trustworthy creation. The sea personified—*Yam*—was the god of the netherworld. And Leviathan was the chaos monster, the one at home in the sea. But not in Psalm 104. The chaotic waters of rebellion or the God of the netherworld? No, just a divine bathtub in which the Lord likes to play with God's bath toys. And Leviathan as the chaos monster? No, God made that thing as a toy in which the Lord takes delight. God's laughter at Leviathan is transformative, re-creative even, shifting the fearful sea monster by means of that divine laughter to an object of creation's goodness.

In each of these cases, when God laughs, that laughter is for a purpose. God's laughter is not merely mocking or derisive, nor is it simply frivolous or silly; God's laughter is powerful. Divine laughter turns the plotting of the evil and the wicked into something that God's people can, in turn, laugh at. Divine laughter makes a joke out of scary things and allows God's people to overcome their fear.

## Laughter in the New Testament

There is, it seems, even less laughter and humor in the New Testament than there is in the Old. "Laugh" in Greek is from the root γελάω (*geláō*), a word that occurs just five times in the New Testament. And those examples are not particularly positive. The author of James goes so far as to discourage laughter: "Lament and mourn and weep. Let your laughter be turned into mourning and your joy into dejection" (Jas 4:9). But then, Luther was right: James *is* an "epistle of straw."[7] We're pretty sure James didn't really have a sense of humor.

Elsewhere in the New Testament, those who laugh do so in disbelief, as in the story of Jairus's daughter: "[Jesus] said, 'Go away; for the girl is not dead but sleeping.' And they laughed at him" (Matt 9:24; see also the parallels in Mark 5:40 and Luke 8:53). Often those who laugh do so in scorn, as at the crucifixion:

> Those who passed by derided him, shaking their heads and saying, "Aha! You who would destroy the temple and build it in three days, save yourself, and come down from the cross!" In the same way the chief priests, along with the scribes, were also mocking him among themselves and saying, "He saved others; he cannot save himself." (Mark 15:29–31)

It is interesting to note that the word for *mock/mocking* in the New Testament, ἐμπαίζω (*empaizō*), is related to the word used in Psalm 104 to describe Leviathan's playing. The word παίζω (*paizō*) is used most often with children, as in to play in a child-like way or to let loose in humor. Paul uses παίζω (*paizō*) in 1 Corinthians 10:7 as he recalls the people of Israel waiting for

Moses to come down from Mount Sinai as they gave in to the idolatry of the golden calf: "Do not become idolaters as some of them did; as it is written, 'The people sat down to eat and drink, and they rose up to play [παίζειν].'" In the Hebrew of Exodus 32:6, the word used is לְצַחֵק (*letsachēq*), which again is from the root word for laugh—but in Exodus 32, the word carries a sexual connotation, as it does in the story of Isaac and Rebekah in Genesis 26. Our droll friends at *The Hebrew and Aramaic Lexicon of the Old Testament* suggest translating the phrase as "and they rose up to amuse themselves wildly."[8] So it seems Saint Paul may not have been against laughter in worship; he was just against orgies in worship.

The only other place that deals with laughter explicitly is Jesus's so-called Sermon on the Plain in Luke 6. There, laughter is promised for those who are weeping now but will be fleeting for those who laugh now:

> Blessed are you who weep now,
>     for you will laugh. . . .
> Woe to you who are laughing now,
>     for you will mourn and weep. (Luke 6:21, 25)

The two types of laughter here are fundamentally different. The first type of laughter we can regard as the "promised laughter of God's preferred future." When God gets busy, Jesus promises, the world will be filled with the joyful laughter of those who have experienced deliverance and redemption. Those who cry now because they suffer with cancer, who weep because they are oppressed and abused, who mourn because they are starving—the air will resound with their redeemed laughter. The second type of laughter we might term as the "present laughter of the earth's self-satisfied." The issue is not simply that those who are happy, healthy, and wealthy now will one day lose everything—and thus that those who laugh now will weep and mourn later. As Mark Allan Powell has written,

> In his parables Jesus depicts the rich as fools who think that the essence of life is to be found in material possessions. . . . God's kingdom brings a reversal of values and call for a reversal of commitments (16:13–15). In this life, those who are faithful to God will divest themselves of material possessions . . . and will be generous to the poor.[9]

Peter Berger noted in his work on humor and theology that "the apparent absence of humor in the sacred texts and in the theology of Christianity create an inconvenient problem for a Christian writer who wants to argue for the religious implications of the comic."[10] But as we have seen, there need not be explicit reference to laughter or humor for both to be bubbling under the surface.

Consider the story from Luke 7 of the woman anointing Jesus's feet with ointment. The story begins,

> One of the Pharisees asked Jesus to eat with him, and he went into the Pharisee's house and took his place at the table. And a woman in the city, who was a sinner, having learned that he was eating in the Pharisee's house, brought an alabaster jar of ointment. She stood behind him at his feet, weeping, and began to bathe his

> feet with her tears and to dry them with her hair. Then she continued kissing his feet and anointing them with the ointment. Now when the Pharisee who had invited him saw it, he said to himself, "If this man were a prophet, he would have known who and what kind of woman this is who is touching him—that she is a sinner." Jesus spoke up and said to him, "Simon, I have something to say to you." (Luke 7:36–40)

There is certainly irony, and we would suggest good humor, in the way Luke tells this story. Simon the Pharisee thinks to himself, "*If* this man *were* a prophet . . ." and Jesus, knowing what is on his mind, addresses him. The irony is twofold: first, in the way that Jesus shows himself to be a prophet—not only knowing that this woman is a sinner but knowing what Simon is thinking—and second, in that Simon does not speak up, but Jesus does. If it is such a problem that a sinful woman is touching Jesus, why does Simon not intervene? Jesus then rebukes Simon for his lack of hospitality by telling a story of not just one but two sinners:

> "A certain creditor had two debtors; one owed five hundred denarii, and the other fifty. When they could not pay, he canceled the debts for both of them. Now which of them will love him more?" Simon answered, "I suppose the one for whom he canceled the greater debt." And Jesus said to him, "You have judged rightly." Then turning toward the woman, he said to Simon, "Do you see this woman? I entered your house; you gave me no water for my feet, but she has bathed my feet with her

> tears and dried them with her hair. You gave me no kiss, but from the time I came in she has not stopped kissing my feet. You did not anoint my head with oil, but she has anointed my feet with ointment. Therefore, I tell you, her sins, which were many, have been forgiven; hence she has shown great love. But the one to whom little is forgiven, loves little." (Luke 7:41–47)

A further irony of the story is that Simon, who sees himself—most likely for reasonable, culturally and religiously appropriate reasons—as a righteous man, is exposed through the honest and selfless behavior of a "sinner" to be a sinner himself. For the one who hears this story, if we can hear it as ironic, or even silly (after all, the reader knows that Jesus is *more* than a prophet), we can chuckle our way through it. More, one can also imagine Jesus himself laughing gently as he finishes his punch line and turns to the woman to say, "Your sins are forgiven."

This business of Jesus as mind reader or heart knower is something of a trope in Luke's Gospel. In addition to the story just mentioned, Jesus knows what people are thinking to themselves four other times, and in at least three cases there is something humorous at play in the stories, or at least bringing humor into our reading of the stories can help us understand them differently and better.

In Luke 5:17–26 Jesus heals a paralyzed man whose friends had committed vandalism and wanton destruction of property to bring him to Jesus. He heals *after* telling them that their sins are forgiven. Jesus perceives the questioning of the scribes and Pharisees in their hearts, and then asks a question: "Which is easier, to say, 'Your sins are forgiven you,' or to say, 'Stand up and walk'?" (Luke 5:23). The healing of the paralyzed man, who at a word from Jesus takes up his mat and walks away laughing in relief and joy at Jesus's punch-line miracle, glorifies God.

In Luke 6:6–11 Jesus is up to his old tricks, healing on the sabbath. He heals a man with a withered hand, despite the fact that the scribes and Pharisees were nearby watching him. Luke tells us that Jesus knew what they were thinking and, once again, he turns to them with a question: "I ask you, is it lawful to do good or to do harm on the sabbath, to save life or to destroy it?" (Luke 6:9). The question might seem innocuous enough, unless we can see how Jesus changes the sabbath expectation from a sort of "pious inactivity" to a "compassionate activity."

In a somewhat different scenario in Luke 9:46–48, Jesus interrupts the disciples' argument about which of them is the greatest, because he is "aware of their inner thoughts" (9:47). He then uses a little child to make his "the least among all of you is the greatest" (9:48) statement. Here there is both the incongruity of a child being "great" and the fact the disciples are, again, arguing about their own greatness [*sic*].[11]

In these stories, the way that Jesus escalates tension with his questions is funny, and once again, it is terribly (read: joyfully) incongruous, as is the way in which he shows up the disciples' foolishness through one of the defining "absurdities" of the gospel—namely, that the greatest are actually those who look like the least, and vice versa (and again, some who are last shall be first, and vice versa [Luke 13:30]).

When it comes to laughter or humor in the New Testament, one might go so far as to say that the relationship between the Testaments is incongruous. Not, mind you, in the simplistic and grossly wrong idea that the God of the Old Testament is different from the God of the New Testament. There is nothing particularly funny about Marcionism. But the truth is that one of the basic ways that the New Testament understands and employs the Old Testament as Scripture is incongruous. Frequently, the way in which the New Testament identifies an Old Testament passage as being "fulfilled" seems, at the least, an unlikely interpretation and, at most, virtually impossible.

Notice how the New Testament begins (at least canonically) in the Gospel of Matthew by apparently getting things wrong, almost right out of the gate. The angelic messenger tells Mary that she will bear a son, and they are to name him "Jesus, for he will save his people" (Matt 1:21) and because the prophet Isaiah promised that "'the virgin shall conceive and bear a son, and they shall name him Emmanuel,' which means, 'God is with us'" (Matt 1:22–24).

Wait, what? Which is it? How can a prophecy that a baby will be named Emmanuel be fulfilled when the baby is named Jesus? *Jesus* doesn't mean "God with us"; it means "Yahweh saves" or "Yahweh is salvation." There's something funny going on here. Was the author of Matthew "half a bubble off level"? Obviously not. Matthew was making the theological point that the Savior who was named Jesus actually is *God with us*. So Jesus fulfills the prophecy in a spiritual rather than literal way. (Sort of like when a baby was born who was supposed to be named Erik but instead was named Rolf because of the constant lobbying of an older sister. *Rolf* means wolf, but we can assure you that he is [al]mostly human.)

## Jesus's Laughter

Does Jesus laugh? As we have said, there may be nothing explicit to draw on in the New Testament, but there is something whimsical and humorous about the way Jesus teaches.

Consider the parables. One old definition of *parable* goes something like this: "A parable is an earthly story, with a heavenly meaning." We have never cared for that definition for two reasons. First, because it is a little too cute and easy. And second, because it is often just backward. If anything, the parables begin with language like this:

> The Kingdom of heaven may be compared to someone who sowed good seed in his field. (Matt 13:24)

Or,

> What is the Kingdom of God like? . . . It is like a mustard seed that someone took and sowed in the garden. (Luke 13:18–19)

Or,

> The Kingdom of God is as if someone would scatter seed on the ground. (Mark 4:26)

These parables ought to be thought of as *heavenly* stories with an *earthly* point, because they speak of God's reign, God's kingdom, and what that means for us here and now. (Not to mention displaying something of an obsession with seeds and sowing.)

A different definition of the parable might be something like this: "A parable is a story with a divine *punch line*."

Many of the parables are crazy sounding, incongruous, and surprising and bear the marks of a good joke with a well-timed punch line. The parables push us to think differently, to conceive of the world and our place in it another way, one that runs counter to typical, earthly thinking but that is in harmony with the gospel.

What sort of shepherd abandons ninety-nine sheep to chase after one? The *good* kind, as it turns out.

What kind of woman, having lost one of her coins, throws a party with it (and who knows how many of the other nine)? The kind who, it seems, is full of the joy of angels.

What kind of father, having watched his son squander his inheritance in all kinds of debauchery, welcomes that son back joyfully? The kind of parent whom God is like, it appears.

We are inclined to agree with what Fredrick Buechner has to say about the parables:

> I think that these parables can be read as jokes about God in the sense that what they are essentially about is the outlandishness of God who does impossible things with impossible people, and I believe that the comedy of them is not just a device for making the truth that they contain go down easy but that the truth that they contain can itself be thought of as comic.[12]

The very purpose of the parables, as laid out by Jesus himself, appears to be counterproductive or, better, counterpurpose. This is teaching that is meant *not* to open everyone up to understanding but to prevent it. According to the Gospel of Matthew, this is the only way that Jesus taught:

> Jesus told the crowds all these things in parables; without a parable he told them nothing. This was to fulfill what had been spoken through the prophet:
>
> "I will open my mouth to speak in parables;
> I will proclaim what has been hidden from the
> foundation of the world." (13:34–35)

And here is how Jesus's parable telling actually works: Jesus said, "The reason I speak to them in parables is that 'seeing they do not perceive, and hearing they do not listen, nor do they understand'" (Matt 13:13). Not only are the parables jokes, of a sort, they are inside jokes. The kingdom of God, then, is for those with a certain sort of sense of humor.

## Jesus *as* God's Laughter: The Incongruity of the Incarnation

If it is true that the key to both humor and theology, outside of the all-important matter of timing, is surprise and incongruity, then Jesus as God's Word made flesh is perhaps the greatest and most surprising incongruity of all.

That the word of God should become flesh is, by itself, an incongruous idea. Indeed, that God should enter into creation by taking on the form of that creation (as the ancient hymn has it, "taking the form of a slave, being born in human likeness"; Phil 2:7) flies in the face of the biblical sense of the relationship between the Creator and the creation. The creation story of

Genesis 1 sees God as outside of or above the creation itself, not "one with it."[13] That the Word that spoke shape and form to what was previously formless and chaotic should himself be spoken *into* that creation, incorporated into it,[14] is novel to say the least. In a sense, the word *incorporate*, if we have a little fun with it, reveals the incongruity and sets up the surprise. If we break down the word incorporate, we get *in-corp-orate*, which we might say means "in-the-flesh-speaking," or "orated into the flesh." Which is, of course, silly nonsense. *But* then is that not precisely the point?

And so the incorporation of the word of Christ—or if you prefer the proper theological lingo, the incarnation—isn't, in the end, the last incongruity. One could imagine a powerful God coming down into the creation, being made manifest and powerful. But the incarnation itself is not the end of God's word, or God's speaking to us in it. The incarnation drives toward the cross, and from the cross to the grave—as the man falling out of the twentieth-story window said as he passed each floor on the way down, "So far so good." But the grave is not the end. The punch line is coming. As we noted in chapter 1, Paul delivers the ultimate gospel punch line in 1 Corinthians 15:

> "Death has been swallowed up in victory."
> "Where, O death, is your victory?
>     Where, O death, is your sting?" (15:54–55)

Or as the Christ hymn of Philippians sings of what comes after obedience, humiliation, and death:

> Therefore God also highly exalted him
>     and gave him the name
>     that is above every name,

so that at the name of Jesus
    every knee should bend,
    in heaven and on earth and under the earth,
and every tongue should confess
    that Jesus Christ is Lord,
    to the glory of God the Father. (2:9–11)

In God's exalting of the Christ, we might hear an echo of the dismissive laughter of Psalms 2, 37, and 59, directed this time not just at the nation's plotting but at the grave's pretention. And at that punch line, every tongue may join in laughing confession. The disbelieving laughter of the outsiders becomes the post-Easter laughter of the faithful. In fact, as the theologian Steve Wilkens has summed the matter up brilliantly, the resurrection of Easter Sunday does not just cancel crucifixion Friday; it forever redefines it:

> Easter redefines crucifixion Friday as Good Friday, it also reframes the suffering, mourning, and tears of that day so that elation, joy, and uncontrollable laughter are appropriate, and in a double sense. It is not just happiness at the reversal of the tragic, but the happy surprise that what seemed so final is not the last word after all.[15]

And thus, he continues, "Shouldn't our spiritual life be infused with joy, laughter, and humor as reminders of the ultimate defeat of suffering and evil?"[16] Yes. Yes, it should.

## The Holy Spirit and the Sense of Humor

In one of the most well-known passages from the Apostle Paul, we are told that there are a variety of spiritual gifts, and a variety of services and activities:

> To each is given the manifestation of the Spirit for the common good. To one is given through the Spirit the utterance of wisdom, and to another the utterance of knowledge according to the same Spirit, to another faith by the same Spirit, to another gifts of healing by the one Spirit, to another the working of miracles, to another prophecy, to another the discernment of spirits, to another various kinds of tongues, to another the interpretation of tongues. (1 Cor 12:7–10)

Or as Paul put it in Galatians, "the fruit of the Spirit is love, joy, peace, patience, kindness, generosity, faithfulness, gentleness, and self-control." Paul concludes, "If we live by the Spirit, let us also be guided by the Spirit" (Gal 5:22–23, 25). The point of these two passages is that the gifts that we have are gifts given us through the work of the Spirit.

Based on our reading of the Old and New Testaments, as well as our sense of the laughter bubbling beneath the surface of much of Jesus's teaching and the divine laughter to which we are invited to add our own voices, we see the sense of humor as another kind of spiritual gift given to us by the Spirit.

In another ironic twist, Job's friend Bildad the Shuhite (one of the shorter people mentioned in the Bible, although the centurion who slept on his watch was even shorter), in trying to help Job make spiritual sense of his trials and tribulations, was so wrong that he might have been right. In Job 8:21 Bildad tells Job, "[God] will yet fill your mouth with laughter, and your lips with shouts of joy." While Bildad's attempts to convince Job of his own guilt probably fell flat, like a joke poorly timed or in poor taste, perhaps what he said was true: God, through the Spirit, will fill our mouths with laughter and our lips with joyful shouts, not because we are blameless or our children sinless and not because we are pure and upright, but because the Spirit delights in giving good gifts to God's people.

What if the Spirit hovering over this all-too-grim creation is the breath that seeks to give rise and voice to laughter?

We do not very often think of God as laughing. But perhaps we should. This will teach us something about ourselves in relation to God. And more importantly, it may give us some critical perspective. As Buechner puts it,

> Is it possible, I wonder, to say that it is only when you hear the Gospel as a wild and marvelous joke that you really hear it at all. Heard as anything else, the Gospel is the church's thing, the preacher's thing, the lecturer's thing. Heard as a joke—high and unbidden and ringing with laughter—it can only be God's thing.[17]

To which we would add our chuckling "Amen!"

# 4

# Who's Laughing Now?

## *Biblical Laughers, Why They Laugh, and a Joyful Homiletic*

God isn't the only one who laughs in the Bible. Plenty of people laugh too. Ironically, some of the people we usually think of as laughing in the Bible don't actually laugh. Think about the story of Noah. You know it. God called Noah—"a righteous man, blameless in his generation" (Gen 6:9)—to build an ark, to save himself and his family from the impending judgment. As the story goes, Noah is building his ark in the driveway, and what do his neighbors make of it all? They laugh at him, of course: "The forecast is clear for days and days, Noah, you great buffoon!" Except they don't laugh at him at all, not in the biblical text. That and other additions to the story come to us by way of the Qur'an (which, if you think about it, is kind of funny in and of itself). But there is laughter and many who laugh in the Bible.

The book of Ecclesiastes suggests that, as with many other things, there is a time for laughter:

> For everything there is a season, and a time for every
> matter under heaven:
> a time to be born, and a time to die;
> a time to plant, and a time to pluck up what is planted;
> a time to kill, and a time to heal;
> a time to break down, and a time to build up;
> a time to weep, and a time to laugh;
> a time to mourn, and a time to dance. (3:1–4)

What follows is a survey of biblical laughers, including reflections on why and how they laugh.

Then, at the end, we offer some ideas about what we are calling "a homiletic of joy." We offer suggestions about how these various examples of biblical laughter can inform our own preaching, as well as help us pursue the bigger question, "What would it look like if our preaching was thoroughly transformed by the idea that God changes the tears of Good Friday into the laughter of Easter Sunday?"

## Who Laughs, and How

There are many who may laugh in the Bible, and they do so in various ways. It is important to note that not all laughter is created equal. There is laughter that is joyful, hopeful, needful; there is also laughter that is hurtful. There is, indeed, a time to laugh, but not necessarily a time for us to laugh in all the ways that we find in Scripture.

Laughter is not restricted to any particular person or people. In general terms, both the enemy and the righteous laugh, as do specific individuals. What follows is (believe it or not) a *brief* survey of biblical laughers and the ways in which they laugh.

### *When Enemies Laugh*

The laughter of the enemy is not uncommon in parts of the Old Testament. Lamentations 1:7 summarizes the nature and the reason for their laughter:

> Jerusalem remembers,
> in the days of her affliction and wandering,
> all the precious things
> that were hers in days of old.
> When her people fell into the hand of the foe,
> and there was no one to help her,
> the foe looked on mocking
> over her downfall.

The enemy laughs, mockingly, when Jerusalem falls. Jeremiah speaks of being made the butt of the enemy's laughter more than once (cf. Jer 20:7). And it is not just external enemies who engage in this behavior; it is internal enemies as well. For example, 2 Chronicles 30 tells the story of King Hezekiah reinstating the Passover festival and summoning all of Judah and Israel to come to Jerusalem to keep the sabbath. In this case, it is the "friend" who is actually the enemy, as most in Israel (the northern kingdom, which Hezekiah does not rule) dismiss his summons: "They laughed them to scorn, and mocked them" (2 Chr 30:10; see also Job 12:4).

And of course, in the New Testament, the enemy laughs at Jesus on several occasions, as he describes Jairus's daughter as "not dead but sleeping" (Mark 5:39–40), and Luke adds, "They laughed . . . knowing that she was dead" (Luke 8:53). After putting Jesus on trial, some mocked him as "King of the Jews" (Matt 27:29–31). And in the moment of his crucifixion, he was mocked by the chief priests, scribes, and elders; by passersby (Matt 27:39–44); and by the others being crucified (both of them, according to Mark and Matthew, but just one of them according to Luke). The "humorous" taunting of God's people and of God's anointed is not uncommon.

Given all the attention to the enemy in the book of Psalms, it should be no surprise that the enemy laughs explicitly quite frequently in the Psalter. Because of the attention on stress, violence, and the frequent victories of the enemy over the psalmist or the psalmist's people, we should expect wicked laughter. Consider, for example, Psalm 80:

> O Lord God of hosts,
>     how long will you be angry with your people's prayers?
> You have fed them with the bread of tears,
>     and given them tears to drink in full measure.
> You make us the scorn of our neighbors;
>     our enemies laugh among themselves. (80:5–6)

Psalm 44 cries out to God that the nation of Israel has been rejected by God; therefore,

> You have made us the taunt of our neighbors,
>     the derision and scorn of those around us.
> You have made us a byword among the nations,
>     a laughingstock among the peoples.
> All day long my disgrace is before me,
>     and shame has covered my face
> at the words of the taunters and revilers,
>     at the sight of the enemy and the avenger. (44:13–16)

These verses are full of mocking, shaming laughter, but most striking is the "laughingstock" of verse 14. The Hebrew phrase translated here as "laughingstock" literally means "shaking of the head," an expression unique to this psalm. The shaking of the head here is associated with "derision" in verse 13, which is the same word used in Psalm 2 to speak of God's laughing at the conspiring of the nations and holding them in derision. Psalm 44 has a full suite of terms for mocking derision: "taunt," "derision," "scorn," "laughingstock," "disgrace," "shame," "revilers." Here are two other examples of similar behavior having to do with the enemy shaking their heads at and mocking the psalmist. The first is found in Psalm 22:

> All who see me mock at me;
> they make mouths at me, they shake their heads;
> "Commit your cause to the Lord; let him deliver—
> let him rescue the one in whom he delights!"
> (22:7–8)

Here, as in Psalm 44, the enemies' head shaking (albeit with a different verb for "shake") is equated with mockery. This, then, might also have something of "laughter" about it. In Psalm 109:25, the enemies shake their heads in scorn:

> I am an object of scorn to my accusers;
> when they see me, they shake their heads.

Mockery and scorn are not the same thing, as scorn here has more to do with offering a reproach, but as with the use of scorn in Psalm 44:13, these parallel concepts seem to come together to form the vocabulary of a certain kind of humor: humor at the expense of another.[1]

It is important to note that there is really only one kind of humor that tickles the fancy of the wicked, and that is the harsh, derisive laughter that reveals contempt. This mocking, scorn-filled laughter at the misfortune of God's people is common; for other examples, see Psalms 25:2; 35:15; 79:4; 123:4. To borrow language from the first Psalm, such laughter is dried up, withered, and withering. Or as the author of Proverbs puts it,

> Like a maniac who shoots deadly firebrands and
> arrows,
> so is one who deceives a neighbor
> and says, "I am only joking!" (26:18–19)

The laughter of the wicked and of the enemies is a type of laughter that the Germans call *Schadenfreude* (those Germans have a word for everything!). Schadenfreude is essentially laughter at other people's failures, defeats, or sufferings—humor at the expense of others. Maybe you recall the two cranky old characters in *The Muppet Show*, Statler and Waldorf. Those two old curmudgeons would only laugh when something bad happened on stage—that's Schadenfreude. Such laughter is inconsistent with following Jesus. As Paul writes, "Rejoice with those who rejoice, weep with those who weep. Live in harmony with one another; do not be haughty, but associate with the lowly" (Rom 12:15–16). Schadenfreude is the laughter of the enemies. It is not the laughter of the righteous.

### *When the Righteous Laugh*

If the wicked seem to laugh somewhat infrequently (though consistently), there is more laughter among the righteous, and far more variety. Before surveying moments when the righteous laugh, a word must be said about who the righteous are. The term *righteous* is not first and foremost a moral term, as we often assume. As Jerome Creach has pointed out in several studies of the term, the "righteous" are those who rely on God. That is, the righteous are neither self-righteous nor self-sufficient. The righteous rely on God for both their righteousness and their daily needs. They pray both "forgive us our sins" and also "give us this day our daily bread" because they rely on God for both the righteousness that comes from divine forgiveness and also the daily life that comes from God's ongoing providence.[2]

Psalm 52:5–7 sees the righteous mirroring, in a sense, the laughter of the enemy. The first four verses of the psalm challenge the behavior of the "mighty one," who plots the destruction of the godly and loves evil more than good and lying more than telling the truth. The psalm then turns to what God will do about all of this, and how the righteous will react:

> But God will break you down forever;
> he will snatch and tear you from your tent;
> he will uproot you from the land of the living.
> The righteous will see, and fear,
> and will laugh at the evildoer, saying,
> "See the one who would not take
> refuge in God,
> but trusted in abundant riches,
> and sought refuge in wealth!" (Ps 52:5–7)

The laughter here is a reflection on the tension, often held up in Scripture, between the behavior of the wicked versus that of the righteous, an observation that is meant to inspire a choice for the righteous path (see Ps 1). Here the idea is that it is laughable to choose the way of the wicked.

But the righteous also laugh in other ways, ways that the enemy does not.

Psalm 126 celebrates a moment or moments in Israel's history when "the Lord restored the fortunes of Zion." It is not exactly clear what moment of restoration the psalm has in mind—perhaps the return from exile, perhaps the rebuilding of the temple, perhaps the reconstruction of Jerusalem wall, or perhaps simply the coming of rain after a season of drought. It is possible that the psalm does not have one particular moment of restoration in mind but rather was composed so that the psalm could be sung at any moment of restoration. The Psalms of Ascent (120–35) were later connected with the Festival of Booths, the fall harvest festival: "You shall keep the festival of booths for seven days, when you have gathered in the produce from your threshing floor and your wine press. Rejoice during your festival . . . for the Lord your God will bless you in all your produce and in all your undertakings, and you shall surely celebrate" (Deut 16:13–15). Psalm 126 may not have been composed specifically for the Festival of Booths, but it came to be associated with that joyful festival:

When the Lord restored the fortunes of Zion,
　　we were like those who dream.
Then our mouth was filled with laughter,
　　and our tongue with shouts of joy;

then it was said among the nations,
"The Lord has done great things for them."
The Lord has done great things for us,
and we rejoiced. (126:1–3)

This psalm is a good example that shows the righteous laughing but not at the expense of others. Instead, the righteous laugh and rejoice in moments of restoration. These moments might include an abundant harvest after a period of drought, a moment of return after a season of exile, a moment of blessing after the experience of loss or curse. Speaking of blessing, the psalm concludes with this blessing:

May those who sow in tears
reap with shouts of joy.
Those who go out weeping,
bearing the seed for sowing,
shall come home with shouts of joy,
carrying their sheaves. (Ps 126:5–6)

This final blessing points to the righteous not just celebrating their own blessings but also rejoicing when others receive blessings and restoration.

The righteous do celebrate their victories, including their military victories. Take, for example, Israel's women celebrating the victory of David and Saul over "the Philistine" in 1 Samuel 18. As David and Saul return victorious to Jerusalem, "the women came out of all the towns of Israel, singing and dancing, to meet King Saul, with tambourines, with songs of joy, and with musical instruments. And the women sang to one another as they made merry" (1 Sam 18:6–7). "Made merry" is from the root word for laughing or making sport.

This joy-filled laughter and good humor that give rise to "merrymaking" are in harmony with the promises of restoration in Jeremiah and Zechariah.

Thus says the Lord,

> I am going to restore the fortunes of the tents of Jacob,
> and have compassion on his dwellings;
> the city shall be rebuilt upon its mound,
> and the citadel set on its rightful site.
> Out of them shall come thanksgiving,
> and the sound of merrymakers.
> I will make them many, and they shall not be few;
> I will make them honored, and they shall not be disdained. (Jer 30:18–19)

And again, in Jeremiah 31:4 we read,

> Again I will build you, and you shall be built,
> O virgin Israel!
> Again you shall take your tambourines,
> and go forth in the dance of the merrymakers.

In both of these cases, the sound and the dance of "merrymakers" have at their heart the sense of laughter.[3] The laughter here is fundamentally different from the Schadenfreude of the wicked. The laughter here is the joyous laughter of the redeemed—laughter at the success of others, laughter at the deliverance of others.

Somewhat differently, the prophet Zechariah promises a restoration in which things "go back to normal":

> The word of the Lord of hosts came to me, saying: Thus says the Lord of hosts: I am jealous for Zion with great jealousy, and I am jealous for her with great wrath. Thus says the Lord: I will return to Zion, and will dwell in the midst of Jerusalem; Jerusalem shall be called the faithful city, and the mountain of the Lord of hosts shall be called the holy mountain. Thus says the Lord of hosts: Old men and old women shall again sit in the streets of Jerusalem, each with staff in hand because of their great age. And the streets of the city shall be full of boys and girls playing in its streets. (8:1–5)

The children will "play," making sport and laughing in the streets.

The power of laughter—of simple, joyful humor expressed in song, dance, and play—is evidenced in many places in the Bible, but the source and the reason for that good humor, whether it is expressed in terms of the enemy getting theirs or in the joy of the restoration of God's favor, are the same: this laughter comes because of what the Lord has done or promised to do. Humor and ROTFLOHO (rolling-on-the-floor-laughing-our-hearts-out) are, according to Scripture, appropriate responses to our God. Perhaps, then, we might say that praise at its core is a matter of the funny bone.

In addition to the general, shared laughter of human beings, there are numerous examples of specific individuals laughing. As we have seen in the previous chapter, God laughs. So too those most well-known biblical laughers, Abraham and Sarah. And there are others.

There is David, leaping and "dancing" (the word might better be translated as "laughing," since it derives from the Hebrew root that means "to laugh" [שחק/*śāchaq*]) before the Ark of the Covenant (1 Chr 15:29) as it comes to Jerusalem. (This and other texts support the notion that worship should include joy and laughter at times.) Note the "capable wife"—better translated as "valorous wife" or "courageous wife" (Prov 31:25)—who laughs in the face of the unknown "time to come" when things might otherwise have been difficult, if not for her stewardship.

The book of Job contains a surprising amount of laughter-talk (more on that later), and there is even an example of the "woman wisdom" of Proverbs 8 engaging in some creative laughter:

> When [God] established the heavens, I was there,
> when he drew a circle on the face of the deep,
> when he made firm the skies above,
> when he established the fountains of the deep,
> when he assigned to the sea its limit,
> so that the waters might not transgress his command,
> when he marked out the foundations of the earth,
> then I was beside him, like a master worker;
> and I was daily his delight,
> rejoicing before him always,
> rejoicing in his inhabited world
> and delighting in the human race. (8:27–31)

The Hebrew in the phrase "rejoicing before him always" might also be translated as something like "laughing because of him all the time." The idea here is that wisdom both participates in and marvels at creation. As God creates in wisdom, wisdom gives forth to joyful laughter, "rejoicing in God's inhabited world."[4]

At this point we should pause for a moment and talk about the question of translation. Thus far we have been using the word "laughter" a great deal. The reason for this is that we want to draw attention to how frequently the root words for "laugh," particularly צחק/שׂחק (*śāchaq/tsāchaq*), actually occur in the Old Testament. That said, when it comes to translating the Bible, we would resist being overly wooden or leaning on a strict one-to-one, as though this word must always be translated as "laugh" or "laughter." As we pointed out in chapter 3 as we dealt with Psalm 104:26 and Leviathan, there are a number of ways in which these words, and this idea, work. The words צחק/שׂחק (*śāchaq/tsāchaq*) indicate not merely laughter but celebrating and rejoicing and even playing, which together give us a rich sense of humor (pun intended) in, with, and under the biblical text.

### *The Laughter of Job*

Laughter in Job has little to do with Job directly. When it comes to laughter, Job does not—is not able to—engage in it but has been reduced to an object and source of laughter:

> I am a laughingstock to my friends;
> I, who called upon God and he answered me,
> a just and blameless man, I am a laughingstock.
> (12:4)[5]

The incongruity of Job's claim and his suffering may reveal a bitter laugh on Job's part. Can a just and blameless man be made a laughingstock? The laughed-at laugher challenges the fairness of it all, "speaking truth to power."

There are two other ways in which laughter is employed in Job. On the one hand, there is the false promise of times of laughter that will come if only Job would admit that his suffering must be the result of his own fault or guilt. Job's friends do not recognize the incongruity of Job's situation but conclude that Job's suffering shows congruity; this is his own fault, and thus God is reproving him. Job's friends are trying to call him back into right relationship with God, and so to "comfort" him, they offer what is either the false promise that he will laugh or the promise of false laughter when he has admitted his guilt. In Job 5, Eliphaz tells Job,

> How happy is the one whom God reproves;
> therefore do not despise the discipline of the
> Almighty.
>
> You shall be hidden from the scourge of the tongue,
> and shall not fear destruction when it comes.
> At destruction and famine you shall laugh,
> and shall not fear the wild animals of the earth.
> (5:17, 21–22)

Eliphaz's message is that if Job accepts his punishment, he will no longer be a laughingstock but will in fact laugh at the possibility of times of trial. This is similar to the comfort offered by Bildad in Job 8:

> See, God will not reject a blameless person,
> nor take the hand of evildoers.
> He will yet fill your mouth with laughter,
> and your lips with shouts of joy. (8:20–21)

The laughter promised in both of these cases is—with the tension of the nature of faithful speech that drives the book of

Job—at best, hollow laughter, wrung not from true joy but from false shame.

In addition to all of this, another striking way that laughter plays a role in Job is in God's responses to Job's accusations. Starting in Job 38, as God "answered Job out of the whirlwind," God points to the wonder of the created order and challenges Job's understanding of his personal situation. We have already seen the parallel constructions of God's laughter and the idea of "playing" with other creatures in Psalm 104:26 and Job 41:5. At the heart of God's response to Job is a menagerie of creation's wonders at which Job may marvel in response to their own joyful "sporting." Running up to the lengthy reflection on the great sea monster Leviathan in chapter 41, God speaks to Job of several animals and asks him if it is by Job's understanding that such things are at play. First there is the "wild ass," which laughs at the city:

> Who has let the wild ass go free?
>     Who has loosed the bonds of the swift ass,
> to which I have given the steppe for its home,
>     the salt land for its dwelling place?
> It scorns [שׂחק/*śāchaq*] the tumult of the city;
>     it does not hear the shouts of the driver.
>         (Job 39:5–7)

Then there is the ostrich:

> The ostrich's wings flap wildly,
>     though its pinions lack plumage.
> When it spreads its plumes aloft,
>     it laughs at the horse and its rider. (Job 39:13, 18)

Next is the horse, which, though laughed at, also laughs:

> Do you give the horse its might?
> Do you clothe its neck with mane?
>
> It laughs at fear, and is not dismayed;
> it does not turn back from the sword.
>
> When the trumpet sounds, it says "Aha!"
> From a distance it smells the battle,
> the thunder of the captains, and the shouting.
> (Job 39:19, 22, 25)

And finally, there is "behemoth," which is perhaps the hippopotamus, and for which we will quote a little more because the description is so much fun:

> Look at Behemoth,
> which I made just as I made you;
> it eats grass like an ox.
> Its strength is in its loins,
> and its power in the muscles of its belly.
> It makes its tail stiff like a cedar;
> the sinews of its thighs are knit together.
> Its bones are tubes of bronze,
> its limbs like bars of iron.
> It is the first of the great acts of God—
> only its Maker can approach it with the sword.
> For the mountains yield food for it
> where all the wild animals play [שׂחק/*śāchaq*].
> (Job 40:15–20)

In each of these cases of the natural playfulness of the animal world and its sheer, joyful wonder, we find God's return challenge to Job. As the case is laid before Job—and us—this becomes a kind of invitation to a humble laughter in response. As we see things "too wonderful" for us, things that are "above" us, we, with Job, may humbly laugh along with the creation, recognizing our place in it; we too are creatures, fearfully and wonderfully made (per Ps 139), and not God.

## Toward a "Homiletic of Joy"

The tastefully named Karl Barth once wrote, "If you have heard the Easter message, you can no longer run around with a tragic face and lead the humorless existence of a man [*sic*] who has not hope. One thing still holds, and only this thing is really serious, that Jesus is the Victor."[6] And who are we to disagree with another Karl? Surely he is correct. The very nature of the Easter gospel message necessitates a certain way of being in the world that includes joy, laughter, and humor. As Steve Wilkens notes, "We are resurrection people, and if elated laughter is not part of our faithful repertoire, I'm not sure we really get Easter."[7] And what's good for the goose (the laity) is also good for the gander (the preacher). If the Christian life is to include joy, humor, and elated laughter, then so also must Christian preaching include joy, humor, and elated laughter.

### *The Laughter of Joy Rather Than Derision, Pride, and Anger*

Not all laughter is created equal. As we have seen, there are different kinds of laughter in the Bible: laughter of surprise, joy, and simple pleasure; laughter that is expressed in song, dance, and play; laughter of derision, ridicule, and scorn; laughter that is a response to new life, restoration, and victory. And these different types of laughter emanate from different types of individuals and groups. The enemy and the righteous both laugh, but they laugh differently and for different reasons.

It should go without saying that the derisive, mocking, disbelieving laughter of the enemy and the unrighteous has no place in the Christian pulpit. But, to be honest, we've heard a lot of preaching, and we've heard some of that derision slip into some Christian sermons.

One of the things to note about the laughter of derision is that it wells forth from the waters of anger and hubris. The derisive person is often full of both anger and pride. And note that both anger and pride are to be numbered amid the seven so-called deadly sins. Who would want to have one's homiletic informed by two of the deadly sins?

Pride or hubris, on the one hand, is about one's mindset and about how one regards oneself and others. Pride defines that mindset that looks down on others and that expects always to be looked up to. Looking down on others is the very definition of contempt or derision. Expecting to be looked up to is an attitude that assumes one is always the smartest person in the room; this is the mindset that doesn't realize one always has more to learn and that even the smartest person in the room has something they can learn from "the least of these." Jokes that belittle others and humor that wells up from a prideful mindset do not belong in the Christian pulpit or in a homiletic of joy. But we've heard some sermons—or rather some laughter and jokes in certain sermons—that have felt awfully close to this sort of derisive humor. Which is, to repeat ourselves, the derisive laughter of the unrighteous.

Anger, on the other hand, is not so much about one's mindset but about one's motivations and emotions. Humor that comes from anger almost inevitably will be humor that tears down rather than builds up; it will be laughter at the expense of others rather than laughter in solidarity with and celebration of others. Anger is an emotion that can serve salutary purposes when it is provoked by specific wrongs that have been committed that hurt people. This kind of anger is instrumental in the sense that this anger exists as a response to a wrong—it exists in order to right the wrong.[8] There is a place in preaching for this type of anger as a reaction to particular crimes and sin. Anger, in this sense, is a helpful "place to visit" but an awful "place to live." Anger might flare up from time to time in one's homiletic, but it should not be the dominant emotional center from which a preacher preaches. Why? Because Christ is risen! Upon further review, death's victory has been overturned. The grave is empty. We rejoice with the company of saints over this good news—which means that laughter and joy rather than anger and sadness ought to be the emotional wells from which the gospel preacher drinks.

The call to preach from a homiletic of joy is especially important today, with the culture wars stirring up anger and division within Christian communities. It is no secret that one way that political parties and their mouthpieces in the media try to motivate their bases is to feed them a constant narrative (usually about their political opponents) designed to stoke anger—apparently, an angry political base is often a motivated political base. As we finish this volume in late 2021, even the Covid-19 pandemic and things such as wearing masks and getting vaccinated have been politicized and polemicized. In such a climate as this, the healing potential for a homiletic of humor and joy is noteworthy. Steve Wilkens has written,

> Humor draws us together and is often the lubricant that allows us to engage in conversation about difficult issues. The reason we enjoy a joke is because it gives life to something within us, and sharing it with another ideally seeks to stir something similar within them that creates an interpersonal bond. In a world where the walls that divide us theologically, culturally, politically, and otherwise seem to get higher and thicker, why doesn't it occur to us to investigate humor as a serious tool for removing deadly barriers and moving toward the unity God wants for Christians? If humor is a love language that brings people together and allows us to build bridges, might it be that we should speak of the God who is the source of love in that same language?[9]

To make one of the central points of this book yet again, we are not saying that sermons should be funny or include jokes. We are actually against jokes in sermons that are simply there as jokes. Preachers who are not funny should not try to be funny. Preachers who are a little funny should not try to be funnier. The purpose of a sermon is to proclaim Christ crucified and resurrected, not to be clever. Rather, preachers should intentionally work to center their preaching in the joy of Christ's resurrection. Preachers should seek to *preach in a register that is attuned to the Easter laughter of new life*. It seems to us that this register will naturally include joy at all times, humor when natural and appropriate, and laughter as a sign of the new life we share in Christ.

A homiletic of joy should also be humble. To state the obvious, humility is the opposite of hubris. If hubris is one of the seven deadly sins, humility is one of the seven cardinal virtues. Much can be said about humility as a virtue, but the primary point is that truly humble preachers point not to themselves in their preaching but to Christ. When it comes to humor and laughter, the humble preacher will rarely be the hero of their own stories in their sermons. The preacher who is always the hero of their own stories will project pride rather than humility. When we were young preachers, we were both taught this important bit of wisdom. An important teacher of ours, James Limburg, modeled this wisdom well. Jim was a wonderful trombone player (that actually may be an oxymoron, but we digress). He is also a jazz aficionado. When he was an undergraduate professor, the great Duke Ellington and his band performed at the college where he taught. After the concert, Jim and his wife, Martha, approached Ellington and asked about his setting of Psalm 150. Ellington then called his trumpet player over, and the two of them played the psalm. (Aside: at the end, Ellington signed an autograph for Martha. "I love you madly!" he wrote.) When Jim writes about this event in his psalms commentary or uses it in a sermon about Psalm 150, he changes the story—taking himself out of the narrative and making it about some anonymous college professor. It is not a terribly important story in itself, but we think it is a good example of a preacher making sure that he is not the hero of his own story. It's a fine example of a properly humble preacher.

A final comment toward thinking about a homiletic of joy. In the New Testament, the apostle writes, "Rejoice in the Lord always; again I will say, Rejoice" (Phil 4:4). And also, "Rejoice always, pray without ceasing, give thanks in all circumstances. . . . Do not quench the Spirit" (1 Thess 5:16–19). Notice that in both of these passages, the point is not joy for joy's sake. The point is that we rejoice *in the Lord*! We rejoice and give thanks as means of letting *the flame of the Holy Spirit blaze without quenching*! The purpose of developing a proper homiletic of joy is that experiencing joy in the Lord is a way of cultivating and practicing the presence of the Holy Spirit. And where the Holy Spirit is present, the joy of the new creation abounds.

# 5

# Wit, Sarcasm, and "Incarnation"

## *Humor and the Prophets*

We turn now to humor in what might seem an unlikely place but is a place that is full of all kinds of humor: the messages of the prophets. Laughter or humor in this case will be less about who is laughing out loud and more about an often-overlooked aspect of the way the prophets communicate and create meaning. As we mentioned earlier, elements of the prophetic material and storytelling about the prophets are amusing; some are clearly intended to be humorous, and others may simply strike one as funny. Recall Elijah showing up the prophets of Baal with his trash-talking, or those ill-mannered children taunting Elisha, or so-called Third Isaiah welcoming the eunuchs into the Temple by telling them they are not just "dry trees," or Jonah, the whole book. Humor of one kind or another is the operative mode of meaning making in the prophetic voice.

## The Wit of Amos: A Case Study of Humor in the Prophets

A professorial wit once remarked, "If you like the prophet Amos, you don't understand him." The professor's point, of course, is that those of us who think we like Amos because he condemns injustice probably miss the fact that if Amos put our lives and "lifestyles" under his prophetic microscope, he would yell, "Icky!" But what if a reader just starts by liking how Amos says what he says? As Peter Berger has written, humor when used as Amos uses it sees "through the facades of ideational and social order and discloses other realities lurking behind the superficial ones."[1] Our point is this: the comic dimensions of Amos's messages are integral, rather than ancillary, to his prophetic witness.

When considering the comic dimensions of Amos's witness, there are several ways to enter in. We begin by looking at two passages in which Amos's rapier wit is evident. We then offer some critical reflection on what sort of wit (or humor) Amos employs and how it functions. Lastly, we will return to the text of Amos and briefly discuss a few other passages in which Amos skewers his prophetic targets.

### *Two Examples of the Prophet's Wit*

We will start with Amos 4:4–5 and invite you to join us in a brief exegetical exercise. Take a moment and read, out loud, the following passage from the prophet Amos:

> Come to Bethel—and transgress;
>     to Gilgal—and multiply transgression;
> bring your sacrifices every morning,
>     your tithes every three days;

bring a thank offering of leavened bread,
and proclaim freewill offerings, publish them;
for so you love to do, O people of Israel! (4:4–5)

We ask you to do this, *out loud*, in order to score a point. The point, which has been made by Donald Juel in an essay entitled "The Strange Silence of the Bible," is that responsible exegesis requires that we read texts aloud. Juel describes the resistance many students have to reading the Bible aloud: "Resistance is great among students who may not know the Bible but have a fixed notion of how it should be read—usually with great reverence and solemnity, but with very little inflection."[2] He continues, "In view of my own experience as a member of congregations where Bible reading is a regular feature of worship and yet is almost never interesting or engaging, I can only applaud such efforts" to experience the biblical text differently.[3] And finally, he says, "Exegesis is [most often] carried on without ever reading aloud, especially in a public setting where one reads and others listen. Actual engagement with the biblical text is an essentially private encounter, done best in a library or study. . . . The Bible is strangely silent among its most devoted students."[4]

Juel's point about reading the text aloud is especially fitting when we approach the prophetic texts. As we well know, the so-called literary prophets, such as Amos, were not authors but speakers. Their prophetic messages were *spoken*, *performed out loud*, to a living audience. And surely the prophets performed their oral message by drawing on the whole range of vocal inflection available. So, in that light, try reading this Amos text again, out loud, this time in a tone that we think is more likely the tone that Amos would have used. Read Amos 4:4–5 in a sarcastic voice:

Come to Bethel—and transgress;
    to Gilgal—and multiply your transgression;
bring your sacrifices every morning,
    your tithes every three days;
bring a thank offering of leavened bread,
    and proclaim free offerings, publish them;
    for so you love to do, O people of Israel!

Now let us turn up the volume on this little vocal experiment to eleven. What sort of life-setting might an interpreter imagine for this passage? The fact that this passage begins with the imperative בֹּאוּ (*bôʾû*), normally translated "come," and is followed in verse 5 by the causal particle כִּי (*kî*), normally translated as "for," suggests that Amos here is offering a prophetic parody of a priestly call to worship, such as the one found in Psalm 95:

O come [בֹּאוּ/*bôʾû*], let us worship and bow down,
    let us kneel before the Lord, our Maker!
For [כִּי/*kî*] he is our God,
    and we are the people of his pasture,
    and the sheep of his hand. (95:6–7; see also
        100:2–4)

An ancient resident of the northern kingdom might well have heard such a call to worship at one of the northern cultic centers, such as Bethel or Gilgal (two of the chief shrines of the northern kingdom), both mentioned in the passage. Notice the pattern. "Come" (בֹּאוּ/*bôʾû*) . . . "for" (כִּי/*kî*). The exact pattern is used in Amos. In other words, Amos here was laying violent hands on a sacral speech form, the call to worship. But, through a bitterly sarcastic parody, he was using the form to condemn rather than commend the people's acts of worship: "For so *you love to do*."

And what setting could one imagine for this parody? James Luther Mays once wrote that this parody of a call to worship "must have been spoken during a festival assembly at Bethel."[5] Mays continues,

> When Amos took up the chanting rhythmic summons "Come ye to Bethel . . . ," the pilgrims would have thought he was one of the cultic functionaries playing his usual role! . . . But hardly had the summons begun than it struck a shocking dissonance: "Come to Bethel!—and rebel!" The Israelites who had come for at-one-ment, to establish peace with their God by sacrificial communion meals and to receive his blessing to secure their welfare, were told that their piety was in fact the very opposite—an offence against, a breach with . . . the God whose community they sought.[6]

While the certainty of Mays's conclusion that this prophetic parody of a call to worship "must" have occurred during the fall festival at Bethel remains in question, we think the proposal is suggestive and fruitful. By imagining this mock call to worship at such a setting, we get a sense of Amos's prophetic wit at work.

As a second example of the prophet's wit, consider Amos 7:7–9 and 8:1–3. These two passages were originally the third and fourth elements in a series of four prophetic vision reports.[7] In the first, Amos reports that the Lord showed him locusts being prepared to descend on the land. Amos cried, "O Lord God, forgive, I beg you!" (7:2). And the Lord relented, "It shall not be" (7:3). In the second report, Amos says the Lord showed him a shower of fire descending to devour both sea and land. Amos cried, "O Lord God, cease, I beg you!" (7:5) And the Lord again relented, "This also shall not be" (7:6).

The interpretation and meaning of the third vision (7:7–9) are disputed. Amos describes seeing a wall being built with what most translations call a "plumb line."[8] For our purposes here, we will stick with this standard translation, since other translations do not change the point we are making. Amos reports seeing the Lord "standing beside a wall built with a plumb line" (7:7). The Lord then announces, "I am setting a plumb line in the midst of my people Israel; I will never again pass them by" (7:8).

This formula is repeated in the fourth vision report (8:1–3), a vision report that turns on a sophisticated pun. Amos announces,

> This is what the Lord God showed me—a basket of summer fruit [קיץ/*qyts*]. He said, "Amos, what do you see?" And I said, "A basket of summer fruit [קיץ/*qyts*]." Then the Lord said to me,
>
> "The end [קץ/*qts*] has come upon my people Israel;
> I will never again pass them by." (8:1–2)

For those readers who read these passages only in vernacular translation, the meaning of these prophetic vision reports is difficult—even impossible—to sort out. Both passages rely on the audience's ability to decipher a pun. In the fourth vision, the pun is more obvious, so we will focus there.

Amos reports seeing a "basket of summer fruit." Since the term "summer fruit" implies the end of the summer growing season with the attending harvest celebrations, the interpreter can assume the image would at first have conjured up favorable associations for an ancient audience. Especially when compared with the images in the first two visions—a menacing cloud of locust and a devouring fire—the image would have seemed remarkably benevolent to the ancients. If so, however, Amos did not allow his audience to linger long in this happy place. In the first two visions, the prophet turned the vision from negative to positive with his proclamation. In the third and fourth visions, he worked his rhetoric the opposite way—turning the vision from positive to negative. The witty hinge on which the prophet worked this rhetorical swing was a pun. The Hebrew word for "summer fruit" was קיץ/*qyts*. Here is a bowl of קיץ/*qyts*, the prophet said, and that is exactly the harvest you have sown and now that you will reap—meaning "the end": "The end [קץ/*qts*] has come upon my people Israel; I will never again pass them by." The fact that the two words are related to different roots only emphasizes the pun.

But there is more than just a simple pun going on here. There is also a bit of cross-cultural awareness and criticism. Research into ancient Hebrew has suggested that regional dialectal differences existed between the Hebrew that Amos spoke—he was from the southern kingdom of Judah—and the Hebrew that his audience in the northern kingdom of Israel spoke. Without diving down into the mind-numbing details (that's what endnotes are for[9]), basically, the idea is that the northern word for "summer fruit" sounded exactly like the word for "the end." We could paraphrase it like this: "What do you northern Israelites call this bowl of *qayits*? That's right, you call it '*qets*.' And you are right—it is 'the end [the *qets*] for you.'" Only in the northern kingdom could the two terms be conflated and punned. Funny, right? Well, maybe the humor gets lost in the translation. That's what our grandparents said when they talked in Norwegian and laughed with each other but wouldn't tell their kids what they were saying.

Puns are the very definition of wit. One definition of "wit" is "a game of intellect and language."[10] Wit, as such, is all about economy of expression. Wit is generally not long-winded. Rather, wit is brief, pithy, apt, to the point. Wit is about one-liners, asides, and puns. One reason that puns qualify as wit—that is, as intellectual humor—is that to make a pun and understand a pun, a large and deep vocabulary is required:

> A large vocabulary in the sense of controlling a great variety of lexemes, often in multiple languages and dialects.
>
> A deep vocabulary in the sense of grasping multiple meanings of any given lexeme—and also of knowing that different languages have different meanings for identical homonyms.

Our point is that Amos's use of a pun in his fourth vision report is a masterful use of just such intellectual humor.

### *Reflections on Amos's Wit*

But what sort of humor is this that Amos employs? And what is its meaning? Or maybe better, what is this humor doing to an audience?

As we have noted above, humor works to diagnose and to challenge reality or perceived reality. To return to Peter Berger's description of humor, it is intrusive—that is, humor almost always has a disruptive element. This seems to be true whether one is considering a joke, a one-liner, a visual caricature, or a lampoon musical number. In the most basic form of a joke—"three so-and-sos walk into a bar"—the first two set the pattern, and the third disrupts the pattern in some way that tickles the funny bone. In a one-liner, the normal grammatical flow of a conversation is disrupted, and so on. What this "intrusive" or "disruptive" quality in humor does is set aside the normal grammar, the normal order of the world momentarily. This momentary setting aside grants an audience a chance to view reality from a new perspective; it allows an audience to see past the disguises and the masks that authorities have composed for themselves. The outcome is that the comic can unmask those things in daily life that are mistaken, or that are deliberately false, or that are immoral, or even that are evil. Berger writes that the comic "seeks to debunk, to unmask. It seeks to show up the pretensions (if one prefers, the false consciousness or the bad faith) of society."[11] And further, Berger says, humor offers

> the insight that things are not as they seem, which further implies that things could be quite different from what is commonly thought. . . . [Comic expressions] establish distance from the world and its official legitimations. . . . Wit debunks. Most of the time this is, as it were, as sociological exercise. That is, it is directed against the pretensions of particular social institutions, conventions, or customs.[12]

## *How Amos's Humor Debunks and Unmasks*

The two examples of Amos's wit that we described earlier are different forms of humor, but both can be said to be doing the work that Berger describes variously as "unmasking," "debunking," "diagnosing," "showing up"—in short, implying that things as they are are not right and that they could be different.

What words fit Amos's use of humor? Parody? Irony? Satire? All the above? The first example, from Amos 4, works by parody. By offering an ironic parody of a sacred speech form—the call to praise/worship—the prophet critiques Israel's worship life and announces God's judgment. The second example, from Amos 8, works by pun. By ironically punning what on the surface seems a benevolent image, the prophet announces the end of forgiveness. With an ominous allusion to the exodus tradition—"I will never again pass them by" (8:2)—the prophet announces the reversal of God's history of mercy.

As Berger notes, satire is "the deliberate use of the comic for purposes of attack."[13] The special targets of the prophet's humorous attacks are those in authority and those others who willingly follow those who are in authority: King Jeroboam, the High Priest Amaziah, the wealthy women of Samaria, and the philosophical and theological leaders (priests and prophets) of Israel. This is how satire works. New dictators often make a priority of shutting down the theaters and comedy clubs when they come into power. As Berger notes, "Dictators have very good reason to suppress satire directed against them."[14] But Berger also points out that "philosophers are only surpassed by theologians in the propensity to take their own theories very seriously, and the comic perspective fundamentally puts all seriousness in question."[15] Thus it should not be surprising that the prophet also targets the priests and prophets.

## *How Amos's Humor Facilitates Consideration of Inconvenient Realities*

A second dimension of the prophet Amos's wit is that humor—by interrupting the normal grammar of daily life—makes it easier for people to look honestly at hard truths, to consider very ugly realities. Precisely because humor works by means of a disruptive, intrusive logic, it interrupts the normal reality in which the polite turn their eyes away from horror, and it destabilizes the fragile balance that we have negotiated wherein we close our eyes to things that make us uncomfortable. Humor, in short, makes it easier to look directly at suffering, to admit that something is indeed wrong with the current regime. Think of how polite society turns its eyes away from the homeless person begging at the bottom of the off-ramp, or how able-bodied society teaches children not to stare at the handicapped or the disfigured, or how great suffering tends to isolate a person.

As Berger writes, "Morally inspired satire must necessarily focus on those regions of darkness."[16] But Berger does not point out that satire also makes it easier to peer into those dark regions. Humor—specifically the sort of gallows humor that Amos uses when he satirically parodies the Israelite funeral dirge to announce to the people that they were dead in their sins—paradoxically spurs people to laugh when they should be crying. The very act of laughing at that which is tragic actually makes it easier to face reality. In the case of Amos, the goal of making it easier for people to face reality and admit the ill health of his society was not the end in and of itself but only the means. Amos's humor drew people's attention to the corruption of the Israelite religion and cult. It helped them consider their own complicity in a rote faith that failed to connect the Lord's holiness to the call for holy living. It fostered in his audience a genuine consideration of the injustice in Israelite society. The end that Amos was shooting for was, of course, societal change. In a word: repentance. Humor is the rhetorical tool Amos used to get people to admit the reality of sin and injustice. And having exposed their sin and injustice, and forcing them to look it square in the eye, Amos called for change: "Take away from me the noise of your songs. . . . Let justice roll down like waters, and righteousness like an ever-flowing stream" (5:23–24).

## Humor as the Seedbed of Hope

A final dimension of Amos's wit—and, frankly, a function of his wit that is easy to overlook amid all the attacking, unmasking, debunking satire—is that the humor points to the pregnant possibility of hope. Or maybe, rather, to a future that may be pregnant with the birth pangs of a new creation.

The ability to laugh in the midst of life's pain is a subversive witness to hope. Even the gallows humor that satirizes villages from which a thousand march out and only a hundred return, or those from which a hundred march out and only ten return, can make laughter a sign of hope in dire circumstances. In short, the ability to express joy in sorrow, laughter in the midst of tears, is a witness to purpose and meaning when so much seems purposeless and meaningless. As Reinhold Niebuhr wrote, "Faith is . . . the final triumph over incongruity, the final assertion of the meaningfulness of existence."[17] For this reason, he also wrote, there is an "intimate relation between humor and faith [that] is derived from the fact that both deal with the incongruities of our existence."[18] Similarly, Berger writes of a "theologically informed sense of humor"—which seems to us an apt description of Amos's wit.[19] Humor interrupts and intrudes on the normal logic and grammar of the world. But it does so in a way that asserts neither meaninglessness nor nihilism but rather—very briefly—a counterlogic, a countergrammar. And for Amos, of course, such a counterlogic was the logic of God, the logic of justice, the logic of righteousness. Berger writes that "the sense of humor is not simply an expression of subjective feelings . . . but rather is *an act of perception pertaining to the reality of the world outside one's own consciousness.*"[20] Humor, by laughing in the midst of crying, by asserting joy in the midst of despair, makes possible an epistemological reversal. Therefore, "the comic is one manifestation of a sacramental universe—a universe that, paraphrasing the *Book of Common Prayer*, contains visible signs of invisible grace."[21] And again, "the comic becomes a great consolation and a witness to the redemption that is yet to come."[22] And, perhaps most strikingly, Helmut Thielicke suggested that if comedy were given a place in theology, it would be in the domain of eschatology.[23]

In the canonical book of Amos, one sees this dimension of humor in the three doxologies that interrupt the series of judgment oracles (4:13; 5:8–9; 9:5–6), in the vision of future hope that ends the book (9:11–15), in the book's witness to the mutability of God (the divine intention is changed twice by intercession, 7:1–6), and in the calls to repent in chapter 5. (Contrary to the expectations of many readers, calls for repentance are not a significant feature of Amos; see 5:14–15, 24.)[24]

## Sarcasm and Other Prophetic Voices

When it comes to that mode of speech that arrives as one of the unwanted gifts of the teenage years—namely, *sarcasm*, which most teenagers think they have invented—Amos may be the prophetic "king" of that sort of comedy, but he is not alone in it. The prophets not only speak for God—solemnly intoning, "Thus says the Lord"—but frequently do so with lips dripping with sarcasm.

In Habakkuk 2, the prophet speaks a trash-talking taunt against any who would oppress or take advantage of others. Habakkuk invites everyone to join in laughing at the foolishness of such wicked oppression:

> Shall not everyone taunt such people and, with
>     mocking riddles, say about them,
> "Alas for you who heap up what is not your own!"
>     How long will you load yourselves with goods
>         taken in pledge? (2:6)

In Ezekiel 24, as Jerusalem is besieged, Ezekiel speaks this taunt to the "rebellious house" of Israel: "The king of Babylon has laid siege to Jerusalem this very day. And utter an allegory to the rebellious house" (24:2–3). Similar to the sarcasm of Amos 4, Isaiah describes a scene in which the prophet is told to speak a message that will not bring understanding:

> Go and say to this people:
> "Keep listening, but do not comprehend;
> keep looking, but do not understand."
> Make the mind of this people dull,
>     and stop their ears,
>     and shut their eyes,
> so that they may not look with their eyes,
>     and listen with their ears,
> and comprehend with their minds,
>     and turn and be healed. (6:9–10)

Try again the exercise of reading this text out loud with sarcasm or even contempt in your voice. The incongruous nature of this warning exposes the foolishness of those whose hearts are hardened to the word of God.

And again, in Isaiah 14, the prophet is invited to sing a taunt song against Babylon. The key verses are 12–15:

> How you are fallen from heaven,
> O Day Star, son of Dawn!
> How you are cut down to the ground,
> you who laid the nations low!
> You said in your heart,
> "I will ascend to heaven;
> I will raise my throne
> above the stars of God;
> I will sit on the mount of assembly
> on the heights of Zaphon;
> I will ascend to the tops of the clouds,
> I will make myself like the Most High."
> But you are brought down to Sheol,
> to the depths of the Pit. (Isa 14:12–15)

These verses are seen by some as a reflection of the legend of the fall of Satan. But when Isaiah calls the king of Babylon "Day Star" and "son of dawn," these are far from references to Satan. The names are shots at the Babylonian king's pride and pomp, and the fleeting nature of his power; his is a star seen early in the morning, but it is quickly gone, obscured by the sun.

Of course, this is not just an Old Testament thing. John the Baptist's prophetic voice surely drips with sarcastic venom as he calls the Pharisees and the Sadducees who have come out for the baptism of repentance a "brood of vipers!" (Matt 3:7). Jesus takes up that phrase as well as he challenged the Pharisees:

> Either make the tree good, and its fruit good; or make the tree bad, and its fruit bad; for the tree is known by its fruit. You brood of vipers! How can you speak good things, when you are evil? For out of the abundance of the heart the mouth speaks. (Matt 12:33–34)

This challenge is almost a parable of sorts and shows up the foolishness of those who think Jesus must be of the devil because he casts out devils.

One more example comes from Paul's letter to the Galatians. As Paul tackles the problem of circumcision and non-Jews who have converted to faith in Christ, a position that caused Paul some trouble with his fellow believers, he takes his opposition to an extreme:

> But my friends, why am I still being persecuted if I am still preaching circumcision? In that case the offense of the cross has been removed. I wish those who unsettle you would castrate themselves! (Gal 5:11–12)

This is Paul trash-talking the circumcision crowd, playfully, and taking the idea to its illogical conclusion.

Reading—or better, *hearing*—sarcasm in the voices of the prophets (and others) can be difficult, and it takes some imagination. But such interpretive imagination will open the text not only for our preaching but for our hearers as well.

## The Prophets as "Incarnational"

The prophets did not just talk the talk as they delivered God's messages; they also walked the walk of that Word. Literally. A striking feature of the prophets and the prophetic message is that the prophet is often, effectively, God's word en-fleshed. This is a different sort of incarnation than that of Christ, of course, but it is a sort of embodiment of the message that is deeper than simple speech. Frequently, the prophet does not simply utter the word the Lord has shown him or her but exemplifies that word in a sort of living metaphor, which is often equal parts tragedy and comedy.

Consider Isaiah 20. As the Assyrian Empire was threatening the kingdom of Judah, the people were looking for allies to keep them safe. They looked to Ethiopia and Egypt for help instead of relying on their God. And so, God's word comes to Isaiah, telling him what he must do: "Go, and loose the sackcloth from your loins and take your sandals off your feet" (20:2). Isaiah then stripped naked and went about his business. For three years. Three years of naked prophetic perambulation. This was to symbolize what would happen to the Ethiopians and the Egyptians, and to bring a realization to the people of Judah. Seeing the naked Isaiah first, and then the fall of Ethiopia and Egypt, the people would say, "See, this is what has happened to those in whom we hoped and to whom we fled for help and deliverance from the king of Assyria! And we, how shall we escape?" (Isa 20:6). The prophet's very life is used to make God's point—namely, that it is folly to trust in any power other than God, that it is laughable to look for help from anyone else. Surely, Isaiah was viewed as crazy, laughed at, and laughed off.

But the shocking method of his delivery would surely have made the message stick.

The prophet Jeremiah embodied God's message similarly, and we will mention just three of the times. First, in Jeremiah 16, the prophet is told that he will not marry and that he will have neither sons nor daughters:

> For thus says the Lord concerning the sons and daughters who are born in this place, and concerning the mothers who bear them and the fathers who beget them in this land: They shall die of deadly diseases. They shall not be lamented, nor shall they be buried; they shall become like dung on the surface of the ground. They shall perish by the sword and by famine, and their dead bodies shall become food for the birds of the air and for the wild animals of the earth. (16:3–4)

The prophet's own life and legacy are symbolic of Judah's fate, because Judah rejected the Lord as his God. Hard. Next, in Jeremiah 13, he is told in effect to put on a dirty diaper, dirty and worthless, and wear it as a symbol of what Judah is to God. Gross. Finally, in Jeremiah 32, there is some hope in Jeremiah's prophetic embodiment of God's word. Jeremiah is told to buy a piece of property from his cousin, to get two deeds signed and paid for—one sealed and one open—and to present them to the scribe Baruch as a symbol of the restoration: "For thus says the Lord of hosts, the God of Israel: Houses and fields and vineyards shall again be bought in this land" (Jer 32:15).

We admit that each of these cases, with the exception of the last, is not, strictly speaking, humorous but rather dark and harsh. It may be that dismissive humor and harsh laughter may have been a response to these prophets and their lives, but the messages themselves are not innately humorous. There is, however, clear theological intrusion that may be helpfully understood through the lens of comedic intrusion. The prophets' messages are meant to shake the people out of their presumed place, out of their expectations of either how things will turn out or how things actually are. A joke of a sort is on them, and they will be surprised both by the setup and by the punch line.

What we see in all of this is that the prophets are far from simple doom and gloom preachers. The prophets often appear to be motivated by their own senses of humor. They see the world in which they minister sideways from other people. This sideways view of the world is, at its root, a humorous one inspired by the divine sensibility that seeks to reestablish world order differently than it is or appears to be now. Unmasking, intruding, debunking, mocking, punning, and so on, the prophets speak the word of the Lord wittily, wryly, even raunchily in order to shake us (mirthfully) out of ourselves.

## From the Prophet's Word to the Preached Word

As we noted at the beginning of this chapter, the prophets were preachers, speaking their messages in real time. With this in mind we could say that, in one sense, the prophetic material is the closest analog for what preachers do. In another sense, the prophets offer the preacher a model for preaching, a model for how to engage God's word. So what can we learn from the prophets and the prophetic penchant for humorous expression?

First, as the prophets at times embodied the Word they were called to deliver, so too can the preacher. By this we don't mean to suggest that preachers should dress in loincloths (or less) and walk around their cities, or spew vitriol all over the newly renovated sanctuary (see Ezek 24). That's been done and we don't condone stealing material. But when it comes to engaging Scripture, and in particular the difficult or challenging passages, the preacher can model the struggle. Not every sermon needs to come across as perfectly polished, and it can be inviting and helpful to the listener if a preacher is honest about the process. If the text challenges you, share that. If a story shocks you or confused you, let it show. Think of this in terms of showing your work on a math problem (although it was our understanding that there would be no math); this can be every bit as helpful for the listener as your having or delivering the "right" answer. Like the prophets, we can embody, publicly, God's word at work in and on us.

Second, and similarly, the preacher can embody the voice of the text. All too often, when Scripture is read, it is done in a flat, toneless voice—the "I'm reading Holy Writ" voice. While this is surely done in order to honor the text, it can rob it of nuance. If a given story has sarcasm, or anger, or joy, read—and then preach—in a similar tone. The way in which we read the text is one of the first opportunities to interpret the text and then to preach it.

Lastly, don't take yourself too seriously. As we noted in the previous chapter, humor and humility can go hand in hand. More, humility can make preaching the difficult message easier, for both the preacher and those who gather to hear the word. It seems to us that the prophets were, for the most part, not too into themselves. Think again of Isaiah, Jeremiah, Hosea, and Ezekiel and all that they were required to endure to preach God's messages, and even John the Baptist with his locusts and his hirsute hair-suit. Jonah took himself too seriously, and look where that got him. While the work we do as preachers is to be taken seriously, we shouldn't take ourselves too seriously. Show some good-humored humility. But only if it's genuine. After all, no one much cares for the guy who thinks he's the very best at being humble.

Oh, and two more notes. First, as you take up the prophetic voice in your preaching, remember what Jesus said about prophets and hometowns—the people who knew you when you ran around in diapers might not be able to take you too seriously. Second, remember that the purpose of so-called prophetic preaching is hope. Walter Brueggemann says the purpose of prophetic ministry is ultimately to reverse the loss of Christian identity in the church today, which has led to "a *ridicule of hope*."[25] True prophetic preaching is not scolding, according to Brueggemann, but Spirit-filled, hope-sparking proclamation that lives "in fervent anticipation of the newness that God has promised and will surely give."[26]

The prophets see the world askance—sometimes what they see and say is pretty funny. But they also see the spirit of God stirring in the world and communicate accordingly. The multifaceted comic dimension of their preaching is integral to their messages. And as those who speak for God in the pulpit, we can take our cues from these ancient preachers and preach rejoicing in fervent anticipation of the new life that God has promised and that the spirit of Christ will surely give.

# 6

# Preach like Peter, Pray like Paul, Laugh like Sarah

*Stand-Up Theologians*

That great biblical sourpuss Qohelet says, "I said of laughter, 'It is mad,' and of pleasure, 'What use is it?'" (Eccl 2:2). And also, "For like the crackling of thorns under a pot, so is the laughter of fools; this also is vanity" (Eccl 7:6). Indeed, it must be admitted that laughter can, at times, seem like madness, particularly in the face of sin, death, and the powers of darkness. What, then, are we to make of this? What are we to make of biblical humor, a humorous reading of the Bible, and our preaching?

At the risk of beating this dead horse as we have been arguing, the Bible is often funny. Laughter, and the sense of humor that gives rise to it, is the first of what we would call "alternative fruits of the Spirit." Love, joy, peace, patience, kindness . . . yes, these are familiar. But Paul's list is only representative, we believe, not exhaustive. There are other spiritual gifts: humor, laughter, sarcasm, and the good nature (read: sense, common decency, and/or base humanity) not to chew with your mouth open.

What is more, humor—and biblical humor in particular—can be life-giving. Neal Brennan has said that telling jokes is like giving air bubbles to a drowning person, a gasp of air that allows him to unscramble things and to keep going.[1] Reading the Bible through a similar lens, and so preaching it, can provide that same life-giving breath of fresh air that may be needed. A homiletical posture that includes humor and that also learns from humorists will preach the texts of the Bible more "fully" and, we believe, more faithfully. So how do we go about it?

## Stand-Ups as Theologians of the Cross

As we said in chapter 1, in their role as truth tellers, stand-up comedians may be favorably compared to theologians of the cross. Comics tell the truth in their own peculiar ways and through their humor alter perception and challenge hearts and minds. Martin Luther said that one deserves to be called a theologian of the cross "who understands the visible and the 'backside' of God [Exod 33:23] seen through suffering and the cross"[2] and who calls a thing what it is. Comedians often do this—they tell the truth about hard things through humor. And so should preachers of the gospel. To quote Peter Berger again, "The sense of humor is not simply an expression of subjective feelings . . . but rather is an act of perception pertaining to the reality of the world outside one's own consciousness."[3] The humorist perceives the world in a particular way—viewing it askance as we have argued—and names his or her perception with almost poetic force.

The theologian of the cross, in a similar vein, perceives God's presence and agency not only in the mountaintop experiences such as at Sinai or the Mount of Transfiguration but also in the deepest moments of suffering, when to normal perception it feels as if God is not present. That is, the theologian of the cross takes the central witness of Christ's crucifixion to be that the place in all history and creation where God was most present and active was in fact the very place in all creation where it seems to normal perception that God cannot be present or active—Christ's suffering and death on the cross. The theologian of the cross then uses that witness as the interpretive lens through which to look for God's ongoing presence and agency in the world. That is, to be clear, the theologian of the cross comes to expect God to show up in the worst moments of suffering. As pastors, we have seen this over and over again. We've seen God's presence in the midst of death, divorce, disability, destruction, and devastation. Every pastor we know has had this experience: They have gone (usually with trepidation) to spend time with a dying saint and their family in a hospice. They pray, read Scripture, listen, empathize, visit, and finally leave. And when they leave, they feel as if it was the dying saint or the family who ministered to the pastor rather than the other way around. Where does that feeling come from? We believe it comes from the to-be-expected presence of the risen Christ even in the saddest moments of suffering and loss. As Berger notes, "The central paradox of the Christian message, as preached by Paul, is the immense tension between the kenotic Christ of the Passion and the *Christus Victor* of Easter morning." And again, "To proclaim this paradox is to engage in an act of folly, as perceived by the wise of the world. In speaking as a fool, the apostle . . . is faithful to the extraordinary character of the message that has been trusted to him . . . [and] he also imitates the weakness assumed by the kenotic savior."[4]

Comedy helps make possible the epistemological reversal that is necessary for the secular imagination to begin to see the kingdom of God that is at hand. The comic experience is transcendent on a lower epistemological level—by pointing out that which is incongruous; comedy relativizes through intrusion the ways in which the dominant epistemology frames reality. It posits, very briefly, that a different social order and epistemological frame are possible. The comic thus suggests that this alternate logic need not be temporary—it doesn't have to end when the laughter ends. But to make the epistemological reversal permanent and redemptive, a different sort of speaker is necessary—the preacher of the gospel. For this reason, Berger can conclude that "perceived in faith, the comic becomes a great consolation and a witness to the redemption that is yet to come."[5]

## Preachers as Stand-Up Theologians

Jerry Seinfeld said, "Being a comedian is like being a murderer; no matter what people tell you, you're probably going to do it anyway."[6] Preaching is like that; preachers are like that. Preachers and comedians (and apparently murderers) have that in common. So, if it is true that preachers have something to learn from stand-up comedians, just what is it that we can take away with us? What follows are several suggestions to keep in mind as we make the move from the text to sermon.

### *Know What You Are Doing*

This first thing we would say is, never mistake the task. As a part of a routine on his Catholic beliefs and going to church, John Mulaney said this: "Then there's the homily . . . the homily is when the priest does a book report that is also stand-up comedy."[7]

A book report that is also stand-up comedy. That there is funny. And, of course, it is also wrong. Preaching is not stand-up comedy, even when it *is* funny. It is important, when comparing preaching and stand-up comedy, to remember that this is not a one-to-one comparison, nor is it imitation of another discipline. The point we are making is that we can learn something both from the humorous portions of the Bible and from the art of the stand-up comic. The goal, of course, it must be made absolutely clear, is *not* to get laughs but to announce that in Jesus Christ, the kingdom of God has come near.

The great comic writer and performer Tina Fey said, "I always wish I could be a stand-up; I tried it, like, three times in Chicago. I remember compared to improv, it was so much scarier and so much more thrilling. 'Cause if you did get a laugh, it was all yours. But then when you were flop-sweaty, that was also all you."[8]

Preachers may sometimes wish they too could be stand-ups, but remember what kind of stand-up you are. When you preach the good news and you see it land, *feel* it change a life as you see it light in someone's eyes, you share in the Spirit's work of saving the lost. And when you blow it, when the sermon just never comes together right and you have to preach it anyway, the Spirit shares in that work too.

Preaching is its own peculiar and vital task, which can and indeed should at times be enlivened with humor. Humor can illuminate the text through an exegetical sensibility that is sensitive to humor, but it is not stand up. In a recent book, Will Willimon reminds us that the most important thing we do is preach:

> Preaching is at the center of pastoral work . . . because of who God is and what God is up to. We know the truth about God only because of the proclamation of one true preacher: Jesus.
>
> The pastor who pleads, "Though I'm not much of a preacher, I am a loving, caring pastor," is lying. There's no way to care for God's people as pastor without loving them enough to tell them the truth about God, what God is up to in the world, and how they can hitch on.
>
> Christianity is a "revealed religion"; it happens when humanity is confronted by a loquacious God. We are unable to think about a Trinitarian God on our own. The truth about God must be revealed, spoken to us as a gift of a God who refuses to be vague or coy. It is of the nature of the Trinity to be communicative, revelatory—the Father speaking to the Son, the Son mutually interacting with the Father, all in the power of the Holy Spirit, God speaking to God's world.
>
> And so a primary means of God's revelation is preaching.[9]

Know what you are doing. You are preaching the gospel of Jesus Christ.

### *You Are Not Trying to Get Laughs; You Are Laughing with Sarah and God*

Not every sermon needs a joke or even a laugh. Not every preacher needs to be funny—in fact, many preachers who try to be, or who force jokes into sermons, need to just stop. We believe no preacher should ever start a sermon with a joke as if you are a high school commencement speaker. Get to the text you are preaching as fast as possible and stick with it.

Let the humor of the text or your own humor be itself. As with a good joke or a good story, the way one tells it can shape whether it really works or not. Good jokes tell themselves, but a good joke can be ruined by a poor joke teller. Something similar is true of the biblical text and is certainly true where the Bible and humor intersect.

That said, the preacher should not be afraid of being funny, of laughing at the often-funny stuff of the life of faith or of the Bible. Laughter—the laughter of joy, of amazement, even of doubt and pain, of Easter morning—is contagious and is a gift that we are called to share with those who hear us. One reason for this is that it is God's very nature to turn both our desperate laughter and our ridiculing laughter into the joyful laughter of the redeemed and forgiven. God loves few things more than turning the scornful laughter of a Sarah into the joyful babbling of a baby named Laughter.

Let's stick with the Sarah story for just a moment, because it is the preeminent story about laughter in the Bible. Sarah laughed at the notion that an old woman, past her childbearing years, could have a baby. True, Abraham also laughed at the promise. But Abraham already had a son (Ishmael), and the promise that Abraham laughed at was about Sarah: "'I will bless her, and moreover I will give you a son by her. I will bless her and she shall give rise to nations; kings of people shall come near from her. . . .' Then Abraham fell on his face and laughed" (Gen 17:16–17). But check out the part of the story when Sarah laughed:

> Now Abraham and Sarah were old, advanced in age; it had ceased to be with Sarah after the manner of women. So Sarah laughed to herself, saying, "After I have grown old, and my husband is old, shall I have pleasure?" The Lord said to Abraham, "Why did Sarah laugh, and say, 'Shall I indeed bear a child, now that I am old?' Is anything too wonderful for the Lord? At the set time I will return to you, in due season, and Sarah shall have a son." But Sarah denied, saying, "I did not laugh"; for she was afraid. He said, "Oh yes, you did laugh." (Gen 18:11–15)

There are a couple of funny things about the story. First, as the text notes, "it had ceased to be with Sarah after the manner of women," meaning she was postmenopausal, no longer menstruating. She could not become pregnant or bear a child. But as Sarah herself notes, Abraham was in a similar place in life: "After I have grown old, *and my husband is old*, shall I have pleasure." The word translated as "pleasure" (Hebrew: *ʿednāh*) occurs only here in the Old Testament, although it is likely related to the name "Eden" (*ʿēden*), thus meaning something like pleasure or bliss. But once again, our comic friends at *The Hebrew and Aramaic Lexicon of the Old Testament* provide the punch line to the joke, defining the word as "lust."[10] Abraham was old, and they hadn't invented Viagra yet. He was not up to having sex, Sarah complained, so there was no sexual pleasure for her. Not only could they not have a child; they couldn't even have sex.

Of course, Sarah laughed. But there is one mistranslation in the NRSV rendering above. The NRSV says, "Sarah laughed to herself." But the Hebrew actually says, "So Sarah laughed in her belly." Sarah didn't laugh quietly to herself. She let out a great big belly laugh. The sort of laugh that reverberates through all of creation. A laugh that came straight from her abdomen, from her belly, *from her womb*—from the source of her pain and agony. As a great professor once preached,

> When God promised her a son, she just tilted her head back and let go a belly laugh to make Abraham's tent quiver.
>
> It was irreverent! Blasphemous! But one thing you'll have to say for it. It did mark the distance between her shriveled, antique hulk—which promised a future only of warts, breast cancer, and a hearing aid—and the word of God. It did mark the difference between the law of genetics and the promise of God. Others might have giggled, tittered, sputtered into their hankies. Not Sarah.[11]

Not Sarah, indeed. Sarah laughed because she was in deep pain. And the laughter was her human response to a God who had made this promise years before. She laughed because God had not delivered.

Until God did. God delivered on the promise. And Sarah delivered a baby boy. In doing so, God did what God does. God turned Sarah's Friday laughter into the joyful laughter of Easter Sunday:

> The Lord dealt with Sarah as he had said, and the Lord did for Sarah as he had promised. Sarah conceived and bore Abraham a son in his old age, at the time of which God had spoken to him. Abraham gave the name Isaac ["he laughs"] to his son whom Sarah bore him. . . . Now Sarah said, "God has brought laughter for me; everyone who hears will laugh with me." (Gen 21:1–3, 6)

And so do we laugh; we laugh with Sarah. And with God. As Chad Bird has written, "But of course God had the last laugh. Or, rather, his divine laughter was infectious. . . . All involved were cracking up, doubling over with delight at how insanely wonderful it all was." And he adds,

> Christianity might have the reputation, in some circles, of being morose and ultraserious, but it is the faith of joy, delight, and—yes—laughter. The seeming impossibility of a ninety-year-old conceiving was followed finally by a virgin conceiving. We shake our heads and smile in wonder. God is up to something. Like a comedian waiting to deliver the punch line, God will eventually deliver the unexpected resurrection. All creation gasps with the happiness of irrepressible joy.[12]

### *Preach with the Theological Equivalent of Comedic Intrusion*

We shared this quotation from Peter Berger earlier, but it bears repeating: "The comic experience provides a distinctive diagnosis of the world. It sees through the facades of ideational and social order, and discloses other realities lurking behind the superficial ones."[13]

Just as comedians see the world askance and intrude with humor into the ideological and cultural realities that lie undiagnosed in front of us, so preachers must learn to see the ideological, cultural, and systemic realities in front of us and intrude with the announcement of the gospel. The offer of the free forgiveness of sins, of the reality of the kingdom of God, and of the power of the Spirit. This is precisely what God's word does.

The gospel is intrusive—it challenges our sense of what is true and upends our understanding of what it means to "have life, and have it abundantly" (John 10:10). What the gospel, and the preaching of it, does is call us into a reimagining of what life and death are really all about and ask us to see that we live accordingly. Preaching that does not take this intrusiveness to heart, and embody it, will never truly be gospel preaching.

We must now go back to the story of Sarah laughing at God one more time. This time, we will hear from Walter Brueggemann regarding Abraham and Sarah's resistance, mockery, and doubt of the promise:

> Abraham, and especially Sarah, are not offered here as models of faith but as models of disbelief. For them, the powerful promise of God outdistances their ability to receive it.
>
> Once again, this story shows what a scandal and difficulty faith is. Faith is not a reasonable act which fits into the normal scheme of life and perception. The promise of the gospel is not a conventional piece of wisdom that is easily accommodated to everything else. Embrace of this radical gospel requires shattering and discontinuity. . . . The gospel promise does not meet them in receptive hopefulness but in resistant

> hopelessness. They have accepted that hopelessness as "normal."[14]

As Brueggemann shows, the gospel promise is intrusive. It breaks into Sarah's hopelessness that she regards as normal and discloses the coming birth of a new creation. The traveling guest responds with a question that is also a promise: "Is anything too wonderful for the Lord?" Brueggemann continues,

> If the question of the Lord is answered, "Yes, some things are too hard, impossible for God," then God is not yet confessed as God. We have not yet conceded radical freedom to God. We have determined to live in a closed universe where things are stable, reliable, and hopeless. If, on the other hand, the question is answered, "No, nothing is impossible for God," that is an answer which so accepts God's freedom that the self and the world are fully entrusted to God and to no other. The question must not be given this answer lightly or easily. The way the story hopes we will answer is to yield utterly to this gracious one, to let the initiative for our lives flow from our hands.
>
> To do the impossible! The gospel in this text reaches beyond our frame of reference. It breaks out of the parameters of reason, wisdom, morality, and common sense. It questions normal epistemology. It shatters accepted value systems. It is the heaviest criticism available about our definitions of reality.[15]

### *Be Truth Tellers, Calling a Thing What It Is*

If preachers are truth tellers, no subject is ever really off-limits in a sermon, as the subject of either laughter or exposition. Race, relationships, politics, money, sex and even sexual violence, language itself, the kingdom of God, the forgiveness of sins, the resurrection of the body—nothing is off-limits.

Dare to "go there." Be willing to take some risks, to tackle the difficult texts, and even to be "edgy." There is an old truism that often gets floated around that the task of preaching is to "comfort the afflicted, and afflict the comfortable" (in our experience, this is usually said by relatively comfortable preachers—such as ourselves). Preachers, like comedians, do need to be willing to take risks. If we ignore the difficult social issues, the hard-to-handle biblical texts, the real unanswered (and perhaps unanswerable) questions of life, the universe, and everything, then we are at least missing out on vital opportunities, and at worse may be derelict in our duty. Humor is a vital tool for entering into risky areas, and we do well to recognize and to use it.

But a caveat: never be arrogant about it. Remember that preaching is not primarily about you. Be prepared to afflict yourself at least as often as you seek to afflict someone else—who is probably less comfortable than you are. And remember that there had better be a payoff, a purpose to the edginess. Discussing the question of whether or not anything is off-limits for a comedian, Robert Klein said, "People ask me, 'Is there anything that's off-limits?' No, but if you do a joke about cancer, it better be funny."[16] In other words, if you are going to "go there," it had better serve the life of faith. And the reality is that congregations may not be as patient or tolerant as they once were. As Bill Burr puts it,

> There's this new level of, like, selfishness when you go to a comedy club . . . where they'll watch you for forty minutes, and take everything as a joke, and then all of a sudden you hit a topic that's sensitive to them, and all of a sudden, you're "making statements." I'm just giving into the fact that once I say something, now it's not mine anymore. It literally goes into somebody else's brain . . . and it's cut with their childhood, their experience, whatever happened that day.[17]

While it may not be right to say that congregations are at a new level of "selfishness," it probably is true that the authority of the preaching office cannot be blithely assumed. There is a contract, of sorts, in the "one-sided conversation" that is preaching that we must do our part to honor. Know this—if "no subject is off-limits," there is a warning as well: "here dwelle dragonnes."

### *Find* Your *Voice*

One of the mistakes we made early on in our careers as preachers was trying to sound like our dad. Our father (now over ninety years old) is still one of the finest preachers we have ever heard. A few years ago, he preached at the funeral of longtime Luther Seminary professor Wendell Frerichs. We were both there. After the sermon—which was elegant, faithful, wonderful, and performative—we turned to look each other in the eye, and we both just shook our heads. Because we knew then and we still know now that we will never preach so well. (Karl started to cry. No wait, that was when he tasted Mom's *lefse* [a Norwegian delicacy] just days after he had made it himself, and finally "gotten it right," and realized he would never make *lefse* as fine as Mom's or preach as well as Dad. For the record, Rolf doesn't even try to make *lefse*.)

When we followed Dad's footsteps into the pulpit (in Karl's case, literally, and in Rolf's case, a little more metaphorically, since steps are a problem for him), we at first—a bit unconsciously but also a bit purposefully—copied his voice. We emulated his study habits, his approach, his style. We even each tried to copy Dad's unusual style of writing his sermons in a very unusual outline form rather than standard sentences and paragraphs. It didn't work. Obviously, we now know. We could certainly have done worse, but we were not genuinely being ourselves.

We also tried at various times early in our ministries to preach like certain of our favorite seminary professors. And we've seen classmates who also tried that. The problem was that we were not preaching in our own voices.

This insight has been shared by numerous comics as they reflect on finding their way. For example, Jerry Seinfeld says, "It's pretty hard to avoid (imitating your influences) when you're just starting, but if you stay with it long enough, that will fall away and you will emerge out of it. That's the goal—to become yourself."[18] Steve Martin puts it like this: "My comedy became more potent as I settled into my own body."[19] And Paul Reiser says, "You really have to find your own style, and it takes a long time. There's really no shortcut; you can't be impatient."[20]

Every comedian we can think of found their own voice and learned to stay in it. Think of Roseanne Barr's wonderfully nasal voice. Or Steven Wright's totally deadpan delivery, or Mitch Hedberg's stoner persona, or Larry the Cable Guy's (totally fake!) southern accent. The list goes on and on. The unique voices of comedians such as Ellen DeGeneres, Gilbert Gottfried,

Norm MacDonald, Sarah Silverman, and so on. All have their own voices. Preachers need this too.

For us, it took years to truly find our own voices. It took practice, trying new things, failing and learning from failure, reverting back to old habits, developing new practices, and listening to those who have to listen to our sermons.

If we could give preachers any advice about how to find their voice, it would be this: Have a conversation with ten or twelve people who listen to you preach regularly, and ask them what you do best in your preaching and what they appreciate most about your preaching. And then *do that more*! You won't get better by working on your biggest weaknesses; they are your weaknesses for a reason. To be you, you have to sound like you and do what you do best.

Here are two examples from times when we were teaching in Luther Seminary's Biblical Preaching DMin program. One woman was a wonderful preacher who had a sentimental and emotional style of preaching—not unlike Frederick Buechner's writing. One classmate, incorrectly offering what he thought would be helpful feedback to one of her sermons, told her to "lose the sentimentality." This classmate was wrong! At first, she mistakenly tried to drop the sentimental voice. It didn't work. She was then encouraged to be herself. And once she settled back into her own voice, this very good preacher became even better. Another woman who was from Canada had a vocabulary that would make Merriam-Webster blush. Some may have wondered who she was trying to impress with such a wide range of words, but she properly refused to change. She wasn't trying to impress anyone; that was simply the way her brain worked: "This is who I am, and I will not drop my vocabulary for anyone."

There is a great story from the Hasidic Jewish tradition about the famous Rabbi Zusya of Hanipos that is helpful here. The story exists in many forms because it was passed down through oral tradition. What follows is one version:

> As Zusya prepared for his own death, one night he had a vision, and he woke up afraid. His students said to him, "What could you have to fear, you who have been as humble, as learned, and as true to God as Moshe Rabenu, Moses our teacher?" Zusya turned to them and said, "I am afraid because in my vision I understood that in the world to come, I will not be asked why I wasn't Moses. I will be asked, why I wasn't Zusya."[21]

We will be judged not on whether we preach like our dad but on whether we preach like ourselves. You do not have to sound like any of the great preachers of our age: Martin Luther King, Billy Graham, or Barbara Brown Taylor. You don't need to try to be more like anyone else. You need to be you as a preacher. And that's a good thing.

### *Go Back to the Well*

Most comedians have recurring bits, pieces they do almost every show they play and that their audiences come to expect and hope for. (Think of Jim Gaffigan's *Hot Pocket* routine, or Ron White's "tater salad" bit.) Preachers can do the same. We are suggesting not that one use the same illustration over and over but that one can use phrasing and body language and even silences to serve as key indicators for the listener that the twist is coming or that the singular point one wishes to make is imminent; this will create expectation (and sometimes hope/relief) in the congregation.

This will take some experimentation, and it will involve failure as a preacher as much as it will success—from sermon to sermon, from congregation to congregation. Over time, the work is as much about trying your "bits" and finding your flow in the give-and-take of the preached and received word as it is about what you have written or prepared. Iliza Shlesinger describes the push-me-pull-me of this interaction beautifully: "It's only in the performing of it that a bit is able to find its voice. People always think I'll stay at home and write, or I'll practice in the mirror; you have to experience the failure, the laughter, where they laugh, why they laugh, why they're not laughing in the same way this time. And you have to do it enough that the nuances become undeniable."[22]

To quote Seinfeld again, "Really good bits go deep into your head, and stay . . . keep coming back." Have a recurring "bit" (a phrase, a flourish, a rhetorical move), and do not be afraid to return to it regularly; this will be a gift and a resource for your hearers.

One of our seminary professors said that most pastors have one good sermon—and that they give it every week. This is both a criticism and a compliment. One of our favorite bishops used to joke about himself as a preacher, "They all say that I only have one string on my fiddle, and I play it all the time." Some preachers really do only have one theological idea that they wrestle out of every text and preach every week. This might be any number of things: God desires social justice, God is with us, God forgives you, God loves you, God wants you to show hospitality to strangers, God wants you to decide for Jesus, and so on. Having only one sermon is not necessarily a good thing.

But we knew another prominent preacher who was beloved for certain stories and themes that he returned to over and over. Sort of like when Tony Campolo tells the "It's Friday, but Sunday's coming" story. Tony knows that he has been hired, in part, to tell that story. People cannot learn a new idea if they do not hear it a number of times (is it eleven times?). They cannot learn a new habit unless they practice it consistently for many days (is it forty days?), and they cannot believe the good news unless it is repeatedly spoken to their dead ears (as in every seven days).

To stretch the one-stringed, musical metaphor to the breaking point, you don't need to play a concert harp; the guitar is good enough, but use all six strings. And play in more than one or two keys—not every song is in G or D.

### *Get Personal*

We were taught in our homiletics courses to avoid getting too personal. We were told to avoid being the hero or the goat of our stories, using "I" too much, or anything that might point to the preacher and, presumably, therefore away from the text. This is an important warning, but one that can be taken too far as well. If our struggles with the text, its meaning and power, are dealt with only as abstractions, then it might be that the gospel will never "come home" for the listener fully. It is OK—and more than OK—to embody in one's preaching the realities of encountering God's intrusive and transformative and humorous word. Steve Martin puts the issue this way:

> "I laugh in life," I thought, "so why not observe what it is that makes me laugh?" And if I did spot something that was funny, I decided not just to describe it as happening to someone else, but to translate it into the first person, so it was happening to *me*. A guy didn't walk into a bar, I did. I didn't want it to appear that others were nuts; I wanted it to appear that *I* was nuts.[23]

When necessary, when appropriate, get personal; show your own struggles, your own insights, your own real faith and salvation working themselves out (Phil 2:12). Model hopeful laughter in the face of troubles, inspired by the humor in the text or in your situation. Your congregation will thank you and join you in it.

There is an old homiletical saying, "Preach from your scars, not your wounds." Each of us have our own wounds and scars. For example, without going into details, when Rolf was fifteen, he was diagnosed with bone cancer and had both legs amputated in a three-year fight with cancer. For the last forty years—a biblical number—he has used a wheelchair. Many of his experiences from cancer and from being disabled can be helpful illustrations when preaching about living the life of faith. As it says in the Psalms, the Lord has "turned my mourning into dancing" (30:11). On rare occasions, some of those stories find their way into his sermons, sometimes with good effect. But not every week! There's nothing worse than being predictable!

### *The Power of Silence*

Sometimes the best thing to do in preaching is to stop talking.

Have you ever noticed how comfortable some comedians are with silence? Some of them will tell a joke or hit a punch line and then just be quiet for what might seem an uncomfortably long time. Johnny Carson used the pause after some jokes, as would Jerry Seinfeld. But nobody could use the long silence better than Norm MacDonald, who sometimes would pause five to six seconds after a joke.

New Testament scholar Craig Koester recently remarked to us that he has learned from a long career of teaching and preaching that people never listen more intently than when he quits talking. When he is preaching along, working with the text, and then suddenly stops talking completely, the silence in the room causes listeners to lean forward and eagerly await the next words. Sometimes silence speaks louder than words, they say. But it is also true that sometimes silence invites listeners to listen more intently.

### *Know When to End*

Finally, good comedians never go on too long. They know when the end of the routine, the monologue, or the sketch has arrived. Too many sermons have several endings—sort of like the long coda on Beethoven's Third Symphony. Yogi Berra said, "When you come to a fork in the road, take it."[24] We say, when you get to the first ending of your sermon, stick the landing and stop. And that seems like a good place to end. May the words of our mouths and the meditations of our hearts be acceptable in God's sight, our rock and our redeemer.

# APPENDIX
## *Two Sermons*

This is not a book about how to use humor or be funny when preaching. It is also not a book of sermons. But we include two sermons here as a way of modeling what we think we have learned about preaching from comedians and from those who study humor. The first, by Karl, was preached at the congregation he serves, Lutheran Church of the Good Shepherd in Minneapolis, Minnesota. It was preached on the occasion of launching a worship series about the challenge of following Jesus. The second, by Rolf, was preached during a daily chapel service at Luther Seminary, where he serves on the faculty. It was preached following two successful surgeries on his then six-month-old son.

### *Skipping Round Stones*

**Mark 9:14–29**

Dearly beloved, grace to you and peace from God our Father and the Lord Jesus Christ. Amen.

Our theme for this fall is "Skipping Round Stones: The Challenge of Following Jesus."

This theme is centered on the idea—the calling, really—of following Jesus, which is, in a sense, rather obvious. After all, isn't that what the Christian life is about at its most basic? And yet sometimes, it seems, the most basic things, the most obvious things, are the things that we can let slide, because we assume them. We take them for granted.

At one of our church council meetings, we posed a simple questions to ourselves: Do you know how to follow Jesus?

One of our council members, a lifelong Lutheran, active and dedicated in every congregation they have been a part of, one of the leaders of this congregation, upon hearing this question flopped back in their chair, dumbstruck. This lifelong Lutheran, this active, dedicated leader of this congregation, didn't know how to answer.

Do you know how to follow Jesus?

Do you know what it means . . . what it takes . . . what it is for . . . what it can do?

Following Jesus is, when we get right down to it, what this whole thing is about.

It is how each of the Gospels really gets going.

In the Gospels, one of the very first things Jesus does is to call "us"—in the biblical narrative it is the first disciples of course, but the call is also to us—to follow.

Take Mark 1:16–17 (see also Matt 4:18–19):

> As Jesus passed along the Sea of Galilee, he saw Simon and his brother Andrew casting a net into the sea—for they were fishermen. And Jesus said to them, "Follow me and I will make you fish for people."

Luke 5:8–11 is a little different.

This is not, right out of the gate, a summons to follow but a description of how Simon Peter came to follow Jesus.

Jesus has just told Simon and the fisherman to cast their fishing nets on the other side of the boat, and the resulting haul was such that "their nets were beginning to break" (Luke 5:6):

> [When] Simon Peter saw [the catch], he fell down at Jesus' knees, saying, "Go away from me, Lord, for I am a sinful man!" For he and all who were with him were amazed at the catch of fish that they had taken; and so also were James and John, sons of Zebedee, who were partners with Simon. Then Jesus said to Simon, "Do not be afraid; from now on you will be catching people." When they had brought their boats to shore, they left everything and followed him. (5:8–11)

John 1:43 is different still. John has both a description of how people come to follow Jesus and a summons from Jesus to follow as well. John the Baptist has baptized Jesus, and the next day, as he is standing with two of his disciples, he sees Jesus:

> and as [John] watched Jesus walk by, he exclaimed, "Look, here is the Lamb of God!" The two disciples heard him say this, and they followed Jesus. (1:36–37)

> The next day Jesus decided to go to Galilee. He found Philip and said to him, "Follow me." (1:43)

This is how the Gospels begin, really get going.
"Follow me," Jesus calls us.
But do we know how to follow Jesus?

Do we know what it means . . . what it takes . . . what it is for . . . what it can do for us, and for the world?

I have been thinking about this, of late, in terms of the metaphor of skipping stones.

Can I assume that we have all skipped stones?

Every child knows that the key to skipping stones is that you need to find one that is flat, ideally smooth as well; a stone that fits in the curve of your hand, one that you can send skimming along the surface of the water, striking parallel to it and making it take flight, once, twice, three times, or more.

But try skipping a round stone and, well, good luck.

Trying to skip a round stone is foolish because it is so much harder to make it go, harder to find the little spot that can catch the water cleanly and lift off. But if you want a challenge, if you want to fly—skip—in the face of what *seems* to make sense to so many, skipping the round stone brings with it the greatest joy.

The life that we are offered in Christ Jesus is like this. It is hard.

The calling to follow is no easy thing. It is difficult.

Perhaps especially now.

In the wake . . . no, the aftermath of a twenty-year war in Afghanistan . . .

In the midst of this ongoing pandemic—the Mu variant now in forty-two countries and forty-nine states . . .

In the face of greater frequency and greater intensity of natural phenomena that disrupt and challenge and take lives . . .

It doesn't matter where we stand politically on any of these issues, on war, or the pandemic or climate change. What

> we can all agree on, I trust, is the human realities that surround us.

There is so much need, so much uncertainty.

And so now, differently than ever, the call to follow Jesus is crucial.

*Not*, mind you, the call to come to church or to read the Bible, or even to pray—though all of these, you understand, are important—*but* the call to follow.

Which brings us, at last, to our reading for worship.

Why didn't we start with Mark 1:16–17 and Jesus's call to follow? Why this story of possession and healing and—let's face it—an exasperated Jesus?

We start our reflecting on following Jesus with this story because it has what is, for my money, one of the most important and accurate descriptions of the reality of the life of faith in all of Scripture.

This man's son is sick, possessed of an evil spirit that makes him unable to speak, and which "seizes him . . . dashes him down; [so that] he foams and grinds his teeth and becomes rigid" (Mark 9:18).

More, it would "often cast him into the fire and into the water, to destroy him" (9:22).

The father then says to Jesus, "If you are able to do anything, have pity on us and help us" (9:22).

I love Jesus's response to this plea. Jesus says, "If you are able!—All things can be done for the one who believes" (9:23).

What, do you imagine, was Jesus's tone of voice when he said that?

Did he say, "If you are able!" patiently, calmly, flatly? Or did he say it in a tone of a disbelief of his own, with a little stank on that "if"?

"*If* you are able!" As if he might go on to say, "Don't you know who you're talking to?"

Daredevil Evel Knievel was once asked as he was preparing to jump the Snake River what he thought his chances of survival were, and he said, "Fifty/fifty." The interviewer then asked him, "If you thought that you had a coin flip's chance of survival, a coin flip's chance that you might die, why do it?" Knievel's response? "Do you know who the hell I am?"

"*If* you are able!" Jesus said. "Do you know who I am?"

When I read this story—and imagine Jesus's response, his tone of voice, his facial expression—I cannot help but laugh. Jesus's response is surprising, and pointed, and hilarious.

But the surprise and the humor of it all don't end with him.

In response to Jesus's wry "*If* you are able!" the boy's father says, "I believe; help my unbelief!" (Mark 9:24).

"I believe; help my unbelief!"

What a great contradiction, what a great irony, what a great *simul*—he both believes and suffers unbelief, all at once.

And so often, this is precisely where we are as well.

*How can we believe now?*

> About wars and abandonment and devastation? About pandemic illness and suffering? About nature's wrath and wreckage?

*What can our belief do now?*

> To stop, to fix, to mend all of these massive problems?

*If we believe, even in our unbelief, how do we follow?*

> It's a lot. It will be hard, if we dare to try it . . .

To follow Jesus is, first, to pray this prayer: "I believe; help my unbelief."

The next? Well, come follow the leader, and see.

*Karl N. Jacobson*
Lutheran Church of the Good Shepherd—September 12, 2021

* * *

## *In Praise of Poop*

You have multiplied, O Lord my God,
your wondrous deeds and your thoughts toward us;
none can compare with you.
Were I to proclaim and tell of them,
They would be more than can be counted. (Ps 40:5)

Then I said, "Here I am, in the scroll is recorded what happened to me."
"I have not hidden your saving help within my heart;
I speak of your faithfulness and salvation.
I do not conceal your love and your faithfulness
from the great congregation." (Ps 40:7, 10; our translation)

Brothers and sisters in Christ . . .

In the Old Testament, when the judge Ehud plunged his short sword into the obese belly of the tyrant Eglon, the sword disappeared, and "it" came out. In the New Testament, when Paul was calculating the balance sheet of gains and losses in the Christian life, he wrote that if we gain Christ, all the losses combined add up to no more than "it." When I was a student here,

Professor Sheldon Tostengard quipped that "it" is the single most underrated human experience. I speak, of course, of poop. And, brothers and sisters in Christ, I rise before you this morning to say this: praise God for poop!

Now I don't praise God for poop in the abstract sense, as if poop in and of itself is anything of great value. After all, poop stinks. It's unpleasant. It's of little redeeming good. But rather, I praise God for poop in more of a functional sense. Because if you don't do it, you will, to borrow a phrase from Shakespeare, "sicken and so die." Which is, after all, why I am praising God. As many of you know, my son Gunnar was born last June 3—six months ago today—with a disease that prevented him from pooping. If that had been the end of the story, Gunnar would have died. But, following successful treatment, including two successful surgeries, Gunnar is alive and thriving, all because—praise the Lord!—he can now poop. So I praise God for the miracle of surgeons, nurses, scientists, medical equipment, and chemicals—God's miracles in the kingdom on the left—all of which made his survival possible. And I praise God for the miracle of the presence of the Holy Spirit, the prayers and support of the body of Christ, and the healing power of God, without which he would have died. And I want to be specific about one thing: it was Gunnar's first surgery last July, the one that gave him a colostomy so that he could poop even if it was into a bag—that was the surgery that saved his life. The second one that patched him all back up, that was merely cosmetic.

The praise of God that I offer before you today is consistent with today's text from Psalm 40 and all of the other psalms of thanksgiving, such as Psalm 30 or Psalm 118. The lament psalms teach us that in times of crisis, we are to turn to God. The thanksgiving psalms teach us that after we come through a time of crisis, we are to come to the public worship of God and give thanks and praise to God for bringing us through the crisis. The author of Psalm 40 said that the Lord had raised her up from the miry bog and set her feet on solid rock. Then she came to worship and told others what God had done for her. She brought a scroll on which she had written down what God had done for her. And she said, "I proclaim your righteousness, faithfulness, and salvation. I do not conceal it in my heart, but I tell of your deeds in the great assembly" (my translation).

The praise of God is not for God's self but for God's mission—praise is for evangelism, for the mutual edification of the community. I am to praise God so that you might know of what God has done for me and so grow in your own faith. And you are to praise God that I might know of what God has done for you and so grow in my own faith. And—according to the book of Psalms—this is supposed to happen in worship. That's what the Bible says. Now it is not by accident that I asked my Christian brother Bill Smith to assist in worship today. Bill is a Baptist, and the Baptists still do this; they have personal testimonies in worship. So the Baptists have faithfully preserved this aspect of biblical worship, more faithfully than we Lutherans. And what we should learn from the Bible is that personal witness and testimony needs to be a part of our congregational life. Maybe it doesn't have to be in worship—but couldn't we do something more intentional in the prayers or in the announcements or maybe squeeze it in after the service before the Vikings kickoff? But we do need to give a place for God's people to praise the Lord for the particular blessings that they have known.

This morning at 3:00 a.m., Gunnar awoke with a diaper that was, to use a biblical word, abundant. It was pressed down, shaken together, running over. And with the psalmist, I said,

You have multiplied, O Lord my God,
your wondrous deeds and your thoughts toward us;
none can compare with you. (Ps 40:5)

And with the psalmist, I now say, "I have not hidden your saving help within my heart; I have spoken of your faithfulness and your salvation; I have not concealed your steadfast love and your faithfulness from the great congregation" (Ps 40:10). Praise the Lord.

*Rolf A. Jacobson*
Luther Seminary Chapel—December 3, 2004

# NOTES

## Introduction

1 For those of you who can't wait, here's one: Who was the greatest comedian in the Bible? Samson. He brought the house down. (Funny, huh? That's what you get for being impatient.)

2 Sermon on Matthew 27:33–56 (1545), in Martin Luther, *D. Martin Luthers Werke* (Weimar: Hermaan Böhlau, 1883–2009), 52:800, quoted in "Martin Luther's Humor," *Word & World* 32, no. 2 (Spring 2012): 140.

3 Rolf Jacobson and Karl Jacobson, "'Everyone Who Hears Will Laugh with Me': Humor and Telling God's Truth," *World & World* 32, no. 2 (Spring 2012): 107–16.

## Chapter 1: A Priest, a Rabbi, and a Pastor Step into a Pulpit

1 See 1 Cor 1:18–25.

2 *Comedians in Cars Getting Coffee*, season 2, episode 6, "Kids Need Bullying," directed and produced by Jerry Seinfeld, featuring Chris Rock, aired July 18, 2013, on Crackle.

3 As Keenen Ivory Wayans put it on *Inside Comedy with David Steinberg*, "I'm a black kid from the projects standing in front of white people from New Jersey—what are we gonna have in common?" *Inside Comedy with David Steinberg*, season 2, episode 5, "Jim Carrey & Keenen Ivory Wayans," aired March 11, 2013, on Showtime.

4 David J. Lose, *Preaching at the Crossroads: How the World—and Our Preaching—Is Changing* (Minneapolis: Fortress, 2013), 3, 5.

5 Jacobson and Jacobson, "'Everyone Who Hears,'" 107.
6 Lose, *Preaching at the Crossroads*, 6.
7 See joke from Sam Kinison, *Breaking the Rules*, directed by Walter C. Miller, aired April 21, 1987, on HBO at "Sam Kinison - Jesus resurrection.avi," posted April 24, 2011, YouTube video, https://www.youtube.com/watch?v=r0c5l45JCyI.
8 Bill Burr, *I'm Sorry You Feel That Way*, directed by Jay Karas, released December 5, 2014, on Netflix, https://www.netflix.com/watch/80004478?.
9 Jim Gaffigan, *Beyond the Pale*, directed by Michael Drumm, aired February 7, 2006, on Comedy Central.
10 Bryan Callen, *Never Grow Up*, directed by John Brenkus, aired October 3, 2017, on Comedy Dynamics Network.
11 Reinhold Niebuhr, *Discerning the Signs of the Times: Sermons for Today and Tomorrow* (New York: Charles Scribner's Sons, 1946), 112.
12 See joke from *Comedy Central Presents*, season 1, episode 6, "Mitch Hedberg," directed and produced by Paul Miller, featuring Mitch Hedberg, aired January 5, 1999, on Comedy Central at "Mitch Hedberg - Bush, search party of 4," posted October 16, 2019, YouTube video, https://www.youtube.com/watch?v=Gj-B1Tng3pQ.
13 Walter Brueggemann, *The Prophetic Imagination*, 40th anniversary ed. (Minneapolis: Fortress, 2018).
14 Brueggemann, 3.
15 Niebuhr, *Discerning the Signs*, 113.
16 Frederick Buechner, *Telling the Truth: The Gospel as Tragedy, Comedy, and Fairy Tale* (San Francisco: Harper & Row, 1977), 53.
17 Louis C. K. in *Talking Funny*, directed by John Moffitt, featuring Ricky Gervais, Jerry Seinfeld, Chris Rock, and Louis C. K., aired April 20, 2011, on HBO.
18 Peter Berger, *Redeeming Laughter: The Comic Dimension of Human Experience* (Boston: De Gruyter, 2014), 34.
19 Martin Luther, "Heidelberg Disputation," in *Luther's Works*, vol. 31, *Career of the Reformer I*, ed. Harold J. Grimm and Helmut T. Lehmann (Philadelphia: Fortress, 1957), 52.

20 Berger, *Redeeming Laughter*, xvii–xviii.

21 Berger, 195.

22 Jacobson and Jacobson, "'Everyone Who Hears,'" 110.

23 Cited in Berger, *Redeeming Laughter*, 215.

24 Ben Johnson and Hugh Holland, eds., *Twelfth Night*, (London: Studio Editions, 1993), 1.5.24, 1.5.54-55.

25 Isaac Asimov, *Asimov's Guide to Shakespeare: A Guide to Understanding and Enjoying the Works of Shakespeare* (New York: Avenel, 1978), 2:18.

## Chapter 2: "I Don't Care Who You Are; That's Funny Right There"

1 Callen, *Never Grow Up*.

2 Ludwig Koehler and Walter Baumgartner, *The Hebrew and Aramaic Lexicon of the Old Testament*, online ed. (Leiden, Netherlands: Brill, 2007), s.v. "מְצַחֵק," published online June 8, 2017, https://dictionaries.brillonline.com/halot.

3 See joke from *Beyond the Pale* at "Burning Bush," posted June 7, 2014, YouTube video, https://www.youtube.com/watch?v=ugTjzCvx76A.

4 Martin Luther, *Luther's Works*, vol. 44, *Christian in Society I*, ed. James Atkinson (Philadelphia: Fortress, 1966), 136.

5 See Donald H. Juel, *Shaping the Scriptural Imagination: Truth, Meaning, and the Theological Interpretation of the Bible*, ed. Matthew Skinner and Shane Berg (Waco, TX: Baylor University Press, 2011).

6 Buechner, *Telling the Truth*, 62. Buechner describes Jesus's parable-joke telling like this: "[Jesus] suggests rather than spells out. He evokes rather than explains. He catches by surprise. He doesn't let the homiletic seams show. He is sometimes cryptic, sometimes obscure, sometimes irreverent, always provocative. He tells stories. He speaks in parables, and though we have approached these parables reverentially all these many years and have heard them expounded upon as grave and reverent vehicles of holy truth, I suspect that many if not all of them were originally not grace at all but were antic, comic, often more than just a little shocking" (62–63).

7 Buechner, 56.

## Chapter 3: "No One's Laughing at God; We're All Laughing with God"

1 Reinhold Niebuhr, *Discerning the Signs*, 111.

2 Niebuhr, 111.

3 Compare Job 9:23, where Job bitterly describes God as laughing mockingly at the suffering of the innocent, and Job 22:19, where Eliphaz, chastising Job, says it is the innocent who laugh mockingly at the calamity of the wicked. See also Pss 44:14 and 79:4, where the people are a "laughingstock."

4 The theme of the wicked being hoisted with their own petard is quite frequent in the book of Psalms. See also Pss 7:14–16; 9:15–16; 10:2; 35:7–8; 63:9–10; 69:21–22; 71:1; 109:20, 26–29; 140:1–3, 9; 141:9–10.

5 For Hebrew wonks, here is Job 41:5a: לְשַׂחֶק־בּוֹ׃ זֶה־יָצַרְתָּ לִוְיָתָן. Compare that with Ps 104: לִוְיָתָן זֶה־יָצַרְתָּ לְשַׂחֶק־בּוֹ׃. Note that the same verb, שחק, follows the same subject, Leviathan.

6 See Jon D. Levenson, *Creation and the Persistence of Evil* (Princeton, NJ: Princeton University Press, 1994).

7 Hey, if you don't like Luther on James, don't get bent out of shape. Luther wrote, "I praise it [James] and consider it a good book." But also, "St. James' epistle is really an epistle of straw, compared to these others [Romans, Galatians, Philippians, etc.]." Martin Luther, *Luther's Works*, vol. 35, *Word and Sacrament I*, ed. E. Theodore Bachmann (Philadelphia: Fortress, 1960), 395, 362.

8 Koehler and Baumgartner, *Hebrew and Aramaic Lexicon*, s.v. "לְצַחֵק," published online June 8, 2017, https://brill.com/view/db/halo.

9 Mark Allan Powell, *Introducing the New Testament*, 2nd ed. (Grand Rapids: Baker Academic, 2018), 175.

10 Berger, *Redeeming Laughter*, 183.

11 See also Luke 11:14–23.

12 Buechner, *Telling the Truth*, 66.

13 Unlike several of Israel's neighbors. The Egyptians, Babylonians, Assyrians, and Mesopotamians all understood the created world and

human beings as being derived, physically, from the gods in some fashion or another. For example, in Babylonian mythology, the world and the heavens were formed from the carcass of the dragon-goddess Tiamat, and human beings were made from a mixture of the god Kingu's blood and clay. Part and parcel of the creation is the divine substance. The Old Testament is critically different at this point.

14 As Martin Luther put it in his explanation to the second article of the Apostles' Creed: "I believe that Jesus Christ, true God, begotten of the Father in eternity, and also a true human being, born of the virgin Mary, is my Lord."

15 Steve Wilkens, *What's So Funny about God? A Theological Look at Humor* (Downers Grove, IL: IVP Academic, 2019), chap. 1, Kindle.

16 Wilkens, chap. 1.

17 Buechner, *Telling the Truth*, 68.

## Chapter 4: Who's Laughing Now?

1 The language of "shaking the head" at someone does not necessarily have a unified or set function throughout the Old Testament, as it is not always clearly associated with laughter. In the psalms cited, it is, as it is in Lam 2:15, where it also has to do with mockery:

> All who pass along the way
> clap their hands at you;
> they hiss and wag their heads
> at daughter Jerusalem;
> "Is this the city that was called
> the perfection of beauty,
> the joy of all the earth?"

In two other cases, Jer 18:16 and Job 16:4, the sense is different, associated with horror in Jeremiah and a kind of superior speech or instruction in Job.

2 See especially Jerome Creach, *The Destiny of the Righteous in the Psalms* (Nashville: Chalice, 2008).

3 For Jeremiah, naturally, this is not all that he has to say about merrymaking. Earlier, in chapter 15, when Jeremiah hears the judgment of the Lord over Judah, that four kingdoms will be given power over the nation, he laments, siding, sorrowfully, with the Lord. Jeremiah says,

> Your words were found, and I ate them,
> and your words became to me a joy
> and the delight of my heart;
> for I am called by your name,
> O Lord, God of hosts.
> I did not sit in the company of merrymakers,
> nor did I rejoice;
> under the weight of your hand I sat alone,
> for you had filled me with indignation. (15:16–17)

4 Earlier in Proverbs, there is a somewhat darker theological tone to the laughter of wisdom, which will only be amused when calamity strikes those foolish ones who have refused to hear the wisdom of God's invitation: "When troubles come, I also will laugh at your calamity; I will mock when panic strikes you" (Prov 1:26).

5 Compare Lam 3:14 and Jer 20:7; 48:26–27.

6 Karl Barth, *Dogmatics in Outline*, trans. G. T. Thomson (New York: Harper & Row, 1959), 23. Cited in Wilkens, *What's So Funny?*, introduction.

7 Wilkens, introduction.

8 Terence Fretheim's reflections on divine anger are helpful here. Terence E. Fretheim, "Theological Reflections on the Wrath of God in the Old Testament," *Horizons in Biblical Theology* 24, no. 2 (2002): 1–26.

9 Wilkens, *What's So Funny?*, chap. 1.

## Chapter 5: Wit, Sarcasm, and "Incarnation"

1 Berger, *Redeeming Laughter*, 34.

2 Donald Juel, "The Strange Silence of the Bible," in *Shaping the Scriptural Imagination*, ed. Shane Berg and Matthew L. Skinner (Waco, TX: Baylor University Press, 2011), 34.

3 Juel, 34.

4 Juel, 35. Juel adds, "For most people in the church, the Bible is part of an oral/aural culture. For scholars, the Bible is studied largely in a silent world" (35).

5 James Luther Mays, *Amos: A Commentary*, Old Testament Library (Philadelphia: Westminster, 1969), 74.

6 Mays, 74.

7 Because this third vision report ends with the book's first announcement against Jeroboam—"I will rise against the house of Jeroboam"—the story of Amos encountering Amaziah (Amos 7:9–17) was inserted after the third vision report.

8 NJPSV notes that "pickax" is another possibility. Donald Gowan notes that the \ to be the Akkadian word for 'tin.' [footnote: Benno Landsberger, "Tin and Lead: The Adventures of Two Vocables," *JNES* 24 (1965): 285–96] But what could be meant by a 'wall of tin' (v. 7) or 'I am setting tin in the midst of my people Israel' (v. 8)?" Donald Gowan, "The Book of Amos: Introduction, Commentary, and Reflections," in *The New Interpreter's Bible*, vol. 7 (Nashville: Abingdon, 1996), 406. Since the word אנך itself means "lead" or "tin," the most likely interpretation is that the term is a synecdoche for the concept of "lead weight on a string" and thus does mean plumb line. See also Mays, *Amos*, 132.

9 For any Hebrew nerds who like to read long philological endnotes: Thus in Judah, hollow roots retained their diphthongs when stressed but contracted when unstressed. So,

| Stressed form | Unstressed form |
|---|---|
| זַיִת | זֵת |
| יַיִן | יֵן |
| מַוִת | מוֹת |
| קַיִץ | קֵץ |

In northern Hebrew, by contrast, one theory is that all hollow roots contracted whether they were stressed or unstressed.

| Stressed form | Unstressed form |
|---|---|
| זֵת | זֵת |
| יֵן | יֵן |
| מוֹת | מוֹת |
| קֵץ | קֵץ |

The inscriptional evidence seems to support this hypothesis, with hollow roots showing as biconsonantal in northern inscriptions. House is *bt* (rather than *byt*) and wine is *yn* (rather than *yyn*). The term "summer fruit" is from the hollow root קיץ, whereas the term "end" is from the geminate root קצץ. Note that in the Gezer Calendar, "one month of summer fruit" is ירח קץ. Likewise, in the Samaria ostraca, a "jug of wine" is נבל ין. See Sandra Landis Gogel, *A Grammar of Epigraphic Hebrew* (Atlanta: Scholars, 1998), 48-49. See also Shalom M. Paul, *Amos: A Commentary on the Book of Amos*, Hermeneia (Minneapolis: Fortress, 1990), 234; James R. Davila, "Qoheleth and Northern Hebrew," *Maarav* 5–6 (1990): 69–87; Daniel C. Fredericks, "A North Israelite Dialect in the Hebrew Bible? Questions of Methodology," *Hebrew Studies* 37 (1996): 7–20; Cyrus Herzl Gordon, "North Israelite Influence on Postexilic Hebrew," *Israel Exploration Journal* 5, no. 2 (1955): 85–88.

10 Berger, *Redeeming Laughter*, 136. "The comic perspective discloses aspects of reality over and beyond the subjectivity of the individual holding the perspective. More specifically, the comic perspective discloses incongruences that are not perceived in the serious attitude . . . laughter can be an opening for truth, but there are instances when this opening is deceptive" (135).

11 Berger, 150.

12 Berger, 152.

13 Berger, 157.

14 Berger, 159.

15 Berger, 33.
16 Berger, 172.
17 Reinhold Niebuhr, *Discerning the Signs*, 130.
18 Niebuhr, 112.
19 Berger, *Redeeming Laughter*, 201.
20 Berger, 208 (emphasis added).
21 Berger, 214.
22 Berger, 215.
23 Berger, 215.
24 Space does not allow for a full consideration of the prophet's rapier wit, but we will point here to a few other examples that may be fruitfully read with humor at hand: the Oracles against the Nations (Amos 1:2–2:16); the Dirge over Virgin Israel (Amos 5:1–3, 16–17); the Call Not to Seek the Lord at Worship (Amos 5:4–7, 10–15); Out of the Frying Pan . . . into the Day of the Lord (Amos 5:18–24); the Cows of Bashan (Amos 4:1–3); the Condemnation of Those Who Lie on Beds of Ivory (Amos 6:1–7).
25 Brueggemann, *Prophetic Imagination*, 11.
26 Brueggemann, 11.

## Chapter 6: Preach like Peter, Pray like Paul, Laugh like Sarah

1 Neal Brennan, *3 Mics*, directed by Neal Brennan, released January 17, 2017, on Netflix.
2 Luther, "Heidelberg Disputation," 31:52 (our translation, with thanks to Hans Wiersma). The normal translation, "the visible and manifest things of God," misses Luther's allusion to Exod 33:23, in which God passes in front of Moses and says, "You will see my backside, but you shall not see my face" (our translation).
3 Berger, *Redeeming Laughter*, 208.
4 Berger, 190.
5 Berger, 215.

6 *Comedians in Cars Getting Coffee*, season 8, episode 1, "Stick Around for the Pope," directed and produced by Jerry Seinfeld, featuring Jim Gaffigan, aired June 16, 2016, on Crackle.

7 John Mulaney, *Kid Gorgeous at Radio City*, directed and produced by Alex Timbers, released May 1, 2018, on Netflix.

8 *Comedians in Cars Getting Coffee*, season 3, episode 5, "Feces Are My Purview," directed and produced by Jerry Seinfeld, featuring Tina Fey, aired January 30, 2014, on Crackle.

9 William H. Willimon, *Leading with the Sermon: Preaching as Leadership* (Minneapolis: Fortress, 2020), 2.

10 Koehler and Baumgartner, *Hebrew and Aramaic Lexicon*, s.v. "עֶעְנָה," published online June 8, 2017, https://brill.com/view/db/halo.

11 Roy A. Harrisville, *Pick Up Your Trumpet* (Minneapolis: Augsburg, 1970), 13.

12 Chad Bird, *Unveiling Mercy: 365 Daily Devotionals Based on Insights from Old Testament Hebrew* (Minneapolis: 1517 Media, 2020), 39.

13 Berger, *Redeeming Laughter*, 34.

14 Walter Brueggemann, *Genesis*, Interpretation: A Bible Commentary for Teaching and Preaching (Louisville, KY: John Knox, 1986), 158–59.

15 Brueggemann, 159.

16 *Comedians in Cars Getting Coffee*, season 4, episode 3, "Opera Pimp," directed and produced by Jerry Seinfeld, featuring Robert Klein, aired July 3, 2014, on Crackle.

17 *Comedians in Cars Getting Coffee*, season 5, episode 3, "Smoking past the Band," directed and produced by Jerry Seinfeld, featuring Bill Burr, aired November 20, 2014, on Crackle.

18 Franklyn Ajaye, *Comic Insights: The Art of Stand-Up Comedy* (Los Angeles: Silman-James, 2002), 199.

19 Steve Martin, *Born Standing Up: A Comic's Life* (New York: Scribner, 2007), 171.

20 Ajaye, *Comic Insights*, 169.

21 See Martin Buber, *Tales of the Hasidim* (New York: Schocken, 1947), 249.

22 *The Comedy Store*, season 1, episode 5, "The Birth of a Bit," directed and produced by Mike Binder, aired October 4, 2020, on Showtime.
23 Martin, *Born Standing Up*, 73.
24 Nate Scott, "The 50 Greatest Yogi Berra Quotes," *USA Today*, March 28, 2019.

# SCRIPTURE INDEX

**1 Corinthians**



**Galatians**



**Philippians**



**1 Thessalonians**



**James**

Working Preacher Books is a partnership between Luther Seminary, WorkingPreacher.org, and Fortress Press.

Books in the Series

*Preaching from the Old Testament* by Walter Brueggemann

*Leading with the Sermon: Preaching as Leadership* by William H. Willimon

*The Gospel People Don't Want to Hear: Preaching Challenging Messages* by Lisa Cressman

*A Lay Preacher's Guide: How to Craft a Faithful Sermon* by Karoline M. Lewis

*Preaching Jeremiah: Announcing God's Restorative Passion* by Walter Brueggemann

*Preaching the Headlines: Possibilities and Pitfalls* by Lisa L. Thompson

*Honest to God Preaching: Talking Sin, Suffering, and Violence* by Brent A. Strawn

*Writing for the Ear, Preaching from the Heart* by Donna Giver-Johnston

*The Peoples' Sermon: Preaching as a Ministry of the Whole Congregation* by Shauna K. Hannan

*Real People, Real Faith: Preaching Biblical Characters* by Cindy Halvorson

*The Visual Preacher: Proclaiming an Embodied Word* by Steve Thomason

*Divine Laughter: Preaching and the Serious Business of Humor* by Karl N. Jacobson and Rolf A. Jacobson

Forthcoming

*For Every Matter under Heaven: Preaching on Special Occasions* by Beverly Zink-Sawyer and Donna Giver-Johnston